# Skills for SUPER WRITERS™

## Grammar • Usage • Mechanics • Spelling

**Program Authors**

Lindamichelle Baron • Sharon Sicinski-Skeans

# Modern Curriculum Press

Parsippany, New Jersey

## Teacher Advisory Board

Loretta Agee
*Curriculum Facilitator*
Minneapolis, MN

Dr. Nancy Livingston
*Professor*
Provo, UT

Laura Summy
*Language Arts Coordinator, K–12*
Weslaco, TX

Teddie Brewer
*Principal*
Las Vegas, NV

DianA Rochon
*Principal*
Chicago, IL

Maureen Tinsley
*Literacy Trainer*
Palm Bay, FL

Dr. Donald Coberly
*Educational Services Coordinator*
Boise, ID

Mary Browning Schulman
*Reading/Language Arts Teacher*
Fairfax Station, VA

Virginia Wiseman
*Writing Specialist*
Wadsworth, OH

Dr. Gerry Haggard
*Director of Reading &
 Language Arts*
Plano, TX

**Project Editors:** Elizabeth Egan-Rivera    Donna Garzinsky    Marianne Murphy    Barbara Noe

**Designers:** Bernadette Hruby    Evelyn O'Shea

## Credits

**Illustrations:** Front cover, stars, 6, 7, 9, 11, 13, 15, 17, 19: Bernard Adnet. 3, 4, 5, 25, 27, 29, 31, 33, 35, 37, 39, 45, 47, 49, 51, 53, 55, 57, 59, 61, 63, 69, 71, 73, 75, 81, 83, 85, 87, 93, 95, 97, 99, 101, 103, 105, 107, 109, 111, 117, 119, 121, 123, 125, 127, 129, 135, 137, 139, 141, 143, 145, 147, 153, 155, 157, 159, 161, 167, 169, 171, 173, 175, 177: Stephen Peringer.

**Photos:** All photos ©Modern Curriculum unless otherwise noted. 19: Raymond Gehman/Corbis. 33: Paul A. Souders/Corbis. 53: ©Renee Lynn/Photo Researchers, Inc. 59, 75: Brian Parker/Tom Stack & Associates. 83: The Stock Market. 87: Adam Woolfitt/Corbis. 101: NASA. 103: Buddy Mays/Corbis. 107: John Cancalosi/DRK Photo. 111: Ulf E. Wallin/The Image Bank. 119: Silver Burdett Ginn. 123: SuperStock, Inc. 125: G.K. & Vikki Hart/The Image Bank. 141: Gary Benson. 147: Prentice Hall. 153: Fotopic/Omni-Photo. 157: SuperStock, Inc. 167: PhotoDisc, Inc. 173: Bonnie Kamin/PhotoEdit.

**Modern Curriculum Press**
An Imprint of Pearson Learning
299 Jefferson Road, P.O. Box 480
Parsippany, NJ 07054-0480
http://www.mcschool.com

1 2 3 4 5 6 7 8 9 10    PO    07 06 05 04 03 02 01 00 99 98

# Contents

## Unit 1: Grammar and Usage: Sentences and Nouns

## Unit 2: Grammar and Usage: Verbs and Adjectives

## Unit 3: Grammar and Usage: Adverbs, Pronouns, Other Parts of Speech

# Unit 4: Mechanics: Capitalization, Abbreviation, Punctuation

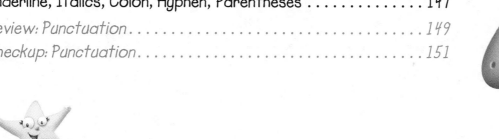

# Unit 5: Spelling

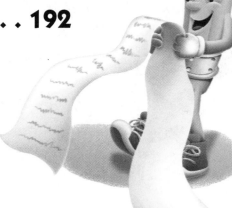

# SUBJECTS

## Become a Super Writer

Juanita is writing a story set at the time of the American Revolution. This is the first sentence of her story.

(Anne) and (Douglas) heard the sounds of horses' hooves.

The **complete subject** in the sentence is underlined. The **simple subjects** are circled. Since there is more than one simple subject, the sentence has a **compound subject**.

> **Definition · Usage**
>
> A **simple subject** is the main noun or pronoun in the complete subject.
> A **complete subject** includes all the words that tell whom or what the sentence is about.
> A **compound subject** has two or more simple subjects that have the same predicate and are joined by the words *and* or *or*.

## Your Turn

**Underline the complete subject of each sentence. Circle all the simple subjects. Circle the first letter of each sentence that has a compound subject.**

1. Anne and Douglas stayed home from school that day.

2. They heard the sounds of a church bell ringing.

3. Anne followed the sounds to the town square.

4. Douglas and their father were close behind.

5. Some men and women were entering the meeting house.

6. Anne, Douglas, and their father went inside, too.

7. A tired messenger announced the good news.

8. The colonies had declared their independence at last.

9. The Founding Fathers had signed the declaration.

10. Many friends and neighbors cheered.

**Use the circled letters to write the last name of a father and son who served as U.S. presidents.**

11. __ __ __ __ __

Juanita added historical facts to her story. Add a complete or compound subject to finish each sentence, using words from the word bank. The clues will help you choose. You'll need to use some words more than once.

| | | | |
|---|---|---|---|
| Bunker Hill | the English | the American patriots | Thomas Gage |
| Yorktown | Breed's Hill | George Washington | bayonets |
| muskets | | Deborah Sampson | |

12. _____ fought against each other in the war. (Clue: two groups of people)

13. _____ commanded the American troops. (Clue: one person)

14. _____ commanded the British soldiers in North America. (Clue: one person)

15. _____ were hills in Massachusetts where early battles took place. (Clue: two places)

16. _____ cut off her hair and disguised herself as a soldier. (Clue: one woman)

17. _____ were among the weapons of the American soldiers. (Clue: two things)

18. _____ spent a long, cold winter at Valley Forge. (Clue: one person and one group of people)

19. _____ surrendered at Yorktown, the war's last major battle. (Clue: one group of people)

**Editing**  Juanita's story ended with a journal entry telling how Anne felt. Add words to the simple subjects to make them more interesting. Circle the compound subject.

| Mistakes | |
|---|---|
| Capitalization | 3 |
| Spelling | 4 |

The war is over! Our new country signed a treaty with England in paris, france. A man told us the news. He rode from Boston. Men, women, and children from all over town gathered in the meting house. The children shouted and ran when they heard the news. We had a party on the village green. Familys came from many miles away. Everywun was happy that the fighting had finally stopped.

# You Understood

## Become a Super Writer

Li is helping to put on an auction to raise money for the public library. She wrote a newspaper ad to announce the auction. The cost is $.50 per word.

*You can come to the library auction. You can bid on great items. You should round bids to the nearest $1.00.*

To save money, Li shortened the sentences in her ad. She noticed that the subject of each sentence was *you*. She knows that *you* will be **understood** even if it is left out of the sentences. This is what she wrote.

*Come to the library auction. Bid on great items. Please round bids to the nearest $1.00.*

**Definition**

In a sentence that gives a command or makes a request, the subject is sometimes left out. The subject is understood to be *you*.

## Your Turn

**Read these sentences from Li's brochure. Write *U* if the subject is *you* understood.**

1. Tell all your friends.  _____

2. Help the library raise money.  _____

3. Li Chang will be the auctioneer.  _____

4. The auction starts at noon.  _____

5. Win a new bicycle.  _____

6. Please donate items for the auction.  _____

7. Mrs. Watts donated a small sailboat.  _____

8. Come to the picnic after the auction.  _____

9. Have lots of fun!  _____

### Auction Price List

| Item | Price | |
|------|-------|---|
| hockey stick | $8.99 | |
| skateboard | $15.00 | |
| wristwatch | $4.75 | |
| CD | $1.95 | |
| football | $7.75 | |
| boomerang | $.85 | |
| tennis racket | $10.50 | |
| radio | $5.75 | |

**Look at the price list to the right. In the third column, round each price under $10 to the nearest dollar. Each rounded price should match the number of a sentence with *you* understood.**

**Add words to make each of the following a sentence with *you* understood. The sentences can tell about Li and the auction, or they can be about something else.**

10. Please _____

11. Look _____

12. Take _____

13. Watch out _____

14. Don't forget _____

15. Try _____

16. Always _____

17. Please don't _____

18. Never _____

19. Call _____

20. Go _____

21. Remember _____

22. Come _____

23. Bring _____

24. Buy _____

25. Give _____

**Editing**  Circle the number of each sentence with *you* understood. Then guess which item each sentence describes. Write your answers on the lines.

| Mistakes | |
| --- | --- |
| Capitalization | 4 |
| Spelling | 8 |

26. I wurk well on Ice. _____

27. Surf the sidwalk with me. _____

28. Don't forget to change my battaries. _____

29. Call me pigskin four short. _____

30. I've got three Hands and a face made of glas. _____

31. I sound grate when i'm spinning. _____

32. Thro me and I'll make a loop. _____

33. i will sirve you well. _____

NAME _____

# PREDICATES

## Become a Super Writer

Adam wants to be an astronomer. He uses his telescope to observe the skies. Here are two of his journal entries.

A meteor (shot) across the sky. Comets (shed) dust and (create) meteor showers.

The underlined part of each sentence is the **complete predicate**. It tells what the subject does. The circled words are **simple predicates**. In the first sentence, the simple predicate *shot* is the main verb in the complete predicate. The second sentence has two simple predicates, *shed* and *create*. This makes it a **compound predicate**.

**Definitions**

The **complete predicate** consists of the simple predicate and all the words that make up the predicate part of the sentence.
A **simple predicate** is the main verb in the complete predicate.
A **compound predicate** consists of two or more simple predicates joined by *and* or *or*.

## Your Turn

**Underline the complete predicates. Circle the simple predicates. Write *C* on the line after each sentence that has a compound predicate.**

1. The space shuttle landed tonight. _____

2. Many clouds blocked my view. _____

3. One star flickered or glimmered dimly last night. _____

4. I read and reread my astronomy magazine. _____

5. I learned many new things. _____

6. The sun contains hydrogen and helium. _____

7. These gases release heat and radiate light. _____

8. The sun's energy warms the earth. _____

9. Solar panels collect sunlight and convert it into energy. _____

10. The moon lights the sky at night. _____

**Underline the simple predicate in each sentence. Then find and circle that predicate in the puzzle.**

11. The astronaut waved his hand.

12. The rocket engines roared.

13. Suddenly, Adam gasped.

14. The space shuttled lifted.

15. The crowd of onlookers cheered.

| g | t | u | c | l | a | r | w | k | d | g |
|---|---|---|---|---|---|---|---|---|---|---|
| a | a | v | l | i | r | o | a | r | e | d |
| v | r | s | a | f | e | d | v | o | y | s |
| e | p | y | p | t | k | i | e | d | a | p |
| y | c | h | e | e | r | e | d | t | u | p |
| x | w | f | b | d | d | p | o | r | w | m |

**Rewrite each sentence above so that it has a compound predicate.**

16. _____

_____

17. _____

_____

18. _____

_____

19. _____

_____

20. _____

_____

**Editing**   Correct the mistakes in Adam's journal. One sentence is missing a verb in the predicate. Add a verb to that sentence.

| Mistakes | Capitalization | 4 |
|---|---|---|
| | Punctuation | 3 |
| | Spelling | 8 |

The earth rotates once every 24 ours. That the lenth of one day, The Planet Venus takes 243 days to rotate. boy, I thought I had a long day! Our galaxy spins in space. it is called the Milky Way. There are so many starz in the galaxy that it looks like a cloud. The sun is just one star out of millyons? Astronomers say there are billions of galaxys! Edwin P. Hubble demonstrated their exiztence in 1923. he used a 100-inch telascope to assist him. I could spend a long time lerning about those galaxies out there

# DIRECT OBJECTS

## Become a Super Writer

Darnel is writing a book called *Famous Firsts*. It tells about people who were the first to do or invent something. Here are two sentences from the book.

Thomas Edison invented the light bulb. He invented it in 1879.

The verb in the first sentence is *invented*. The **direct object**, *light bulb*, answers the question "What was invented?" In the second sentence, *it* is the direct object. The pronoun *it* refers to what was invented.

**Definition**

The **direct object** receives the action of the verb in the sentence. The direct object may be a noun or a pronoun.

## Your Turn

**Underline the verb in each sentence. Then write the direct object on the line.**

1. Marie Curie discovered radium. _____

2. Anthony Gatto juggled seven flaming torches. _____

3. Neil Armstrong visited the moon. _____

4. The Wright brothers flew an airplane. _____

5. The Chinese invented paper. _____

6. Roald Amundsen explored the South Pole. _____

7. Amundsen had high hopes for his trip. _____

8. Ethiopians made the first stone tools. _____

9. They used them for digging, eating, and hunting. _____

10. Jackie Joyner-Kersee won three Olympic gold medals. _____

11. Jonas Salk found a vaccine for polio. _____

12. Alexander Graham Bell patented the first telephone. _____

13. James Naismith invented basketball in 1891. _____

14. The athletes played the first game with a soccer ball. _____

Darnel had to write a fiction story for homework. Help him complete his assignment by writing a direct object on each blank line. Choose from the direct objects in the word bank.

| cat | her | word | sentence |
| --- | --- | --- | --- |
| volume | dog | paragraph | hair |
| CD | video | it | tape |

Christopher sat at his computer for hours. He hadn't yet typed a single

(15) _____ . It was getting late, and the story was due the next morning. He had

waited until the last minute. His mother called to him, but he didn't hear (16)_____ .

He played a (17)_____ . He adjusted the (18)_____ . He combed his

(19)_____ . But he could not think of anything to write. Finally Christopher typed

one (20)_____ . He thought about it for a few minutes. Then he deleted

(21)_____ . He petted the family's black (22)_____ . It purred, but it didn't

have any ideas either.

 **Editing**   Correct the mistakes in the end of Darnel's story. Five of his direct objects are misspelled.

| Mistakes | |
| --- | --- |
| Capitalization | 4 |
| Punctuation | 3 |

Finally Christopher got an ideah. He typed a few wurds. then he typed a few

sentenses sentences became paragraphs, and paragraphs sprouted chapturs.

Getting the first few words on paper started the ideas bubbling Before long,

pages were streaming from christopher's printer! Soon he had more than twenty

sheats? He yelped with joy when he read his story. It was about a boy who had

waited until the last moment to start a story. it began, "Christopher sat at his

computer for hours."

# INDIRECT OBJECTS

## Become a Super Writer

Monique makes greeting cards. She sells them to friends and people at school. She makes lists to stay organized. Here are items from one list.

Send <u>Mrs. Davis</u> the new card. Write <u>her</u> a thank-you note.

In the first sentence, the word *card* is the direct object. It receives the action of the verb *send. Mrs. Davis* is the **indirect object**. She is the person to whom the card is being sent. In the second sentence, the pronoun *her* is the indirect object. The thank-you note is being written to *her*.

**Definition**

An **indirect object** tells to whom or for whom the action was done.

## Your Turn

**Look at the items on Monique's list. Underline the direct object in each sentence. Circle the indirect object.**

1. Send Tom an E-mail message.

2. Give him a list of customers.

3. Get Evan some colored computer paper.

4. Show Lisa the new design.

5. Send Ann her first batch of cards.

6. Offer Susie a special deal.

7. Lend Tina the camera.

8. Give Dad a sample birthday card.

9. Read Alice the new greeting.

10. Teach Yvette the art program.

11. Write Orin a letter.

12. Then tell friends the good news.

**Use the first letter of each indirect object above to solve this riddle.**

13. What unofficial holiday is celebrated each year by school children?

___ ___ ___ ___ ___ ___ ___ ___ ___ ___ ___ ___ school

Complete these sentences. For each, choose a verb from the word bank, then think of an indirect object to add. Write your answers on the lines. You may need to change the form of the verb.

| write | send | give | tell | teach |
|-------|------|------|------|-------|
| bring | pay | sing | read | lend |

14. I will _____ _____ a book.

15. Jamie _____ _____ a song.

16. Please _____ _____ your new bicycle.

17. Dad will _____ _____ a birthday present.

18. _____ _____ a nursery rhyme.

19. Jed will _____ _____ an invitation.

20. Rick, _____ _____ a joke.

21. They should _____ _____ the money they owe.

22. Margo should _____ _____ a letter.

23. Please _____ _____ some fresh bread.

 **Editing**    Monique is designing a card that lists thoughtful things to do for others. Rewrite each sentence. Change each indirect object to refer to one of your friends or relatives.

| Mistakes | |
|----------|---|
| Capitalization | 4 |
| Spelling | 7 |

24. Give somone a Gift. _____

25. send a frend a postcard. _____

26. Make a Grandparent a card. _____

27. Reed someone a storey. _____

28. thank a parent for something. _____

29. Teach a yunger person sumthing. _____

30. Help someone with something. _____

31. Bring someone somthing. _____

# PHRASES

## Become a Super Writer

Peter loves to eat. He is writing a report on what to eat for a healthful diet. Here are his notes about the food-guide pyramid.

at the base—foods from grains

When Peter started to write his report, he knew he needed to turn the phrases into sentences. This is what he wrote:

        adjective        verb            adverb
Foods from grains may be found at the pyramid's base.

The underlined groups of words in these sentences are phrases. Notice that a phrase can act as an adjective, a verb, or an adverb.

**Definition**

> A **phrase** is a group of words that has meaning but that does not express a complete thought.

## Your Turn

**Use the clues in parentheses to find and underline the phrase in each sentence. Two sentences have two phrases.**

1. The tip of the pyramid shows fats, oils, and sweets. (adjective phrase)

2. You should eat these foods sparingly. (verb phrase)

3. Milk and cheese come from animals. (adverb phrase)

4. Children should drink milk daily. (verb phrase)

5. Cholesterol is present in all animal foods. (adverb phrase)

6. A cup of yogurt is a good source of calcium. (adjective phrases)

7. French fries should not be eaten often. (verb phrase)

8. Breads and cereals are foods from grains. (adjective phrase)

9. Vegetables are sources of fiber. (adjective phrase)

10. Foods from plants supply vitamins and minerals. (adjective phrase)

11. Sugars come from ice cream and from heavy syrups. (adverb phrases)

**Circle the numbers of the sentences with two phrases, and write them below.**

12. A healthful diet includes ___ to ___ servings of bread, cereal, rice, and pasta each day.

**Add a phrase to each sentence. The phrase can act as an adjective, a verb, or an adverb.**

13. I eat pizza often. _____

14. I like bread, too. _____

15. Get some exercise. _____

16. Do not use salt. _____

17. Drink skim milk. _____

18. Consume less sugar. _____

19. Cut away the fat. _____

20. Butter has calories. _____

21. Spinach is a vegetable. _____

22. Use low-fat dressing. _____

**Editing** Peter created a menu based on the food guide pyramid. Correct the six misspelled words. Underline one verb phrase, double-underline one adjective phrase, and circle one adverb phrase.

| Mistakes | |
|---|---|
| Capitalization | 2 |

Breakfast is my first and favorite meal of the day. I start this meal with sereal and milk. I drink a glass of orange juis. For lunch I eat a tunafish sandwich. I enjoy a piece of frute for desert. I usually drink a glass of skim milk with each meal. for dinner I start with a large salad. Then I have chicken and vegetables as a main coarse. For dessert I have strawberries with creem. Meals like these taste good. They include foods from each level of the food guide pyramid. eating the right amount of food from each group should make for a healthful diet.

# CLAUSES

## Become a Super Writer

Roberto uses an atlas to explore. Read this sentence from his journal.

The highest mountain in North America is Mount McKinley, which I would like to climb some day.

There are two **clauses** in this sentence. One clause is underlined. Notice that it states a complete thought. The other clause is circled. This clause is not a complete thought. It cannot stand alone.

### Definition · Usage

A **clause** is a group of words that has a subject and a predicate.
A clause that can stand alone is an **independent clause**.
A clause that can't stand alone is a **dependent clause**. It may begin with words like *which, who,* or *that.*

## Your Turn

**Underline each dependent clause in the following sentences from Roberto's journal. Circle the words *which, who,* or *that.***

1. The Grand Canyon is the most exciting place that I have ever seen.

2. The Colorado River was mapped by explorers who were very brave indeed.

3. One was John Wesley Powell, who had lost an arm in the Civil War.

4. The largest freshwater lake in the world is Lake Superior, which is one of the Great Lakes.

5. Niagara Falls is one sight that I really must see someday.

6. I'd also like to visit the Everglades, which is a huge swamp in Florida.

7. There's sawgrass in the Everglades that grows twelve feet high.

8. I'm also curious about the wildlife that remains in the Everglades.

9. A world atlas was published in 1808 by John Cary, who was born in England.

10. I use the atlas that was published in 1998.

**Label each clause as *dependent* or *independent*, using the lines provided. Edit the independent clauses to add periods (⊙) and capital letters (≡).**

11. who is an arm-chair traveler now _____

12. Roberto wants to be a travel writer someday _____

13. which is an island in Florida _____

14. the southernmost point in the United States is Key West _____

15. which was settled by the French _____

16. many tourists are attracted to New Orleans, Louisiana _____

17. boat trips through the bayous are taken by many visitors _____

18. who come to New Orleans _____

19. which is in Bar Harbor, Maine _____

20. Cadillac Mountain is part of Acadia National Park _____

21. Thunder Hole is a popular site _____

22. that tourists like to visit _____

23. in his journal, Roberto makes a list of places _____

24. that he wants to visit and write about _____

**Editing**  Read Roberto's description of New York City. Circle the five dependent clauses.

| **Mistakes** | | |
|---|---|---|
| Capitalization | 3 |
| Punctuation | 2 |
| Spelling | 5 |

New york is one of the greatest cities in the world. In 1619 the Dutch settled the city, which is maid up of five boroughs. Native Americans sold Manhattan Island to Peter Minuit, who was one of the settlement's first guverners. The settlers got a real bargain with the $24 worth of trinkets that Governor minuit pade. New York, whitch was than called New amsterdam, grew rapidly It continued to grow for three centuries. Today the city attracts people who come from all over the world. Some come as tourists, but many also come to live and to work?

# SENTENCE PARTS

**Underline the complete subjects of these sentences. Write the simple subjects on the lines.**

1. Colonial girls covered their heads with cloth caps. _____

2. Young women began to wear bonnets in the 1700s. _____

3. Large hats with decorations were popular in the 1800s. _____

**Underline the complete subject in each sentence. Write the compound subjects on the lines.**

4. Most men and women now wear hats for protection. _____
   _____

5. Helmets and hard hats are two examples. _____ _____

6. Football players and construction workers wear them.
   _____ _____

**Underline the complete predicates of these sentences. Write the simple predicates on the lines.**

7. Young Navy men wore flat-topped hats long ago. _____

8. Pictures of them appeared in magazines. _____

9. People called these hats "boaters." _____

**Underline the complete predicate in each sentence. Write the compound predicates on the lines.**

10. People today like baseball caps and wear them everywhere.
    _____ _____

11. Baseball caps look good and protect the face. _____
    _____

**Write _You_ before each sentence in which the subject is _you_ understood.**

_____ 12. Always wear some kind of hat on cold winter days.

_____ 13. Much of your body heat escapes through the top of your head.

_____ 14. Cover your head on hot sunny days in summer.

**Underline the direct object in each sentence. Circle the indirect object.**

15. We're buying our friends some souvenirs.

16. That little shop sells tourists all kinds of hats.

17. Let's get Jimmy the hat with the helicopter blades.

18. Get Susan that visor with the bow.

19. I'll buy Peter that black hat with the big ears on it.

20. Let's send Grandma a postcard while we're here.

**Read the underlined phrase in each sentence. Write *adjective, adverb,* or *verb* to tell what kind of phrase it is.**

21. Everyone <u>is wearing</u> baseball caps these days. _____

22. You see these caps <u>on the heads</u> of people old and young. _____

23. Very few hats work well <u>with ponytails.</u> _____

24. Baseball caps <u>can be worn</u> with long or short hair. _____

25. The brim <u>of the cap</u> shields the face from the sun. _____

26. Some people turn the brims of their caps <u>toward the back.</u> _____

27. Baseball caps <u>with logos</u> are popular. _____

**Write *phrase* or *clause* on the line to label each group of words.**

28. under the bed _____

29. who designed the hat _____

30. should have been worn _____

31. that the hat maker ordered _____

32. with the wide brim _____

**Underline the dependent clauses in these sentences. Circle the words *who, which,* or *that* in each clause.**

33. Many sports require head coverings, which are worn for safety.

34. Bike riders and other cyclists wear helmets that protect their heads.

35. Helmets are worn by people who play football and other sports.

36. Some jobs have hats that are associated with them.

37. Firefighters wear hats that are hard and protect against fire.

# SENTENCE PARTS

Read each sentence. Choose the answer that tells which part of the sentence is underlined. Fill in the circle.

1. Giraffes <u>eat leaves from the tops of tall trees.</u>

   ○ complete predicate     ○ compound predicate     ○ simple predicate

2. Their long <u>necks</u> help the giraffes reach food.

   ○ simple subject     ○ complete subject     ○ compound subject

3. <u>Wild animals</u> have adapted to their environment to survive.

   ○ simple subject     ○ complete subject     ○ compound subject

4. Giraffes <u>bellow, grunt, and give off</u> short flutelike notes.

   ○ complete predicate     ○ compound predicate     ○ simple predicate

5. Giraffes <u>gallop</u> by moving both legs on the same side together.

   ○ simple subject     ○ complete subject     ○ simple predicate

6. <u>Giraffes and elephants</u> are the tallest land animals.

   ○ simple subject     ○ complete subject     ○ compound subject

Find the compound subject for each sentence. Fill in the circle by your answer.

7. Hedgehogs and porcupines have quills for protection.

   ○ porcupines, quills     ○ hedgehogs, porcupines

   ○ porcupines, protection     ○ protection, quills

8. Insects, snakes, and birds' eggs make up a hedgehog's diet.

   ○ snakes, eggs, hedgehog's     ○ snakes, birds, eggs

   ○ insects, snakes, eggs     ○ insects, snakes, birds'

9. People and other animals have learned to avoid this pincushion of a hedgehog!

   ○ people, pincushion     ○ people, animals

   ○ pincushion, hedgehog     ○ other, pincushion

**Read each sentence. Fill in the circle by the one in which the subject is *you* understood.**

10. ○ Wild animals can amaze you.

   ○ Don't take anything they do for granted.

11. ○ Elephants are really awesome animals.

   ○ Make your friends laugh with elephant jokes.

**Find the direct object in each sentence. Fill in the circle by your answer.**

12. The elephant uses its muscular trunk for many purposes.

   ○ elephant      ○ muscular      ○ trunk      ○ purposes

13. This huge animal drinks water with its trunk.

   ○ huge      ○ animal      ○ water      ○ trunk

14. The powerful trunk can uproot an entire tree.

   ○ powerful      ○ trunk      ○ entire      ○ tree

**Find the indirect object in each sentence. Fill in the circle by your answer.**

15. Can you tell me the Swahili word for *trip*?

   ○ you      ○ me      ○ for      ○ trip

16. I will give you a big hint.

   ○ I      ○ give      ○ you      ○ hint

17. Send me a postcard from your safari.

   ○ send      ○ me      ○ postcard      ○ your

**Read each sentence. Fill in the circle by the answer that tells which part of the sentence is underlined.**

18. The trunk <u>of the African elephant</u> has two "fingers" at its tip.

   ○ adjective phrase      ○ verb phrase      ○ adverb phrase

19. Elephants have tusks, <u>which are like long incisors.</u>

   ○ adjective phrase      ○ verb phrase      ○ clause

20. A frightened elephant <u>will spread</u> its ears.

   ○ clause      ○ verb phrase      ○ adverb phrase

21. Most elephants live <u>in small family groups.</u>

   ○ adjective phrase      ○ verb phrase      ○ adverb phrase

# SIMPLE, COMPOUND, AND COMPLEX SENTENCES

## Become a Super Writer

Barry keeps a birdwatching journal. Here is what he wrote this morning.

*Wild birds flock to my feeders. I enjoy watching them.*

Both sentences are **simple sentences**. Each expresses a complete idea. Barry could have combined the two ideas in a **compound** or a **complex sentence**. He could have written:

*Wild birds flock to my feeders, and I enjoy watching them.* (compound sentence)

*When wild birds flock to my feeders, I enjoy watching them.* (complex sentence)

### Definitions · Usage

A **simple sentence** expresses one complete thought. It may have more than one subject and more than one predicate.
A **compound sentence** has two or more simple sentences that are joined by a comma and a conjunction, such as *and, but, or, nor, for,* or *so.*
A **complex sentence** includes a simple sentence and one or more clauses that cannot stand alone.

## Your Turn

**Read these sentences from Barry's journal. Write *simple*, *compound*, or *complex* to identify each sentence.**

1. Downy woodpeckers are shy birds. _____

2. Birds fly around my head while I fill the feeders. _____

3. Goldfinches squabble over seeds, but juncos feed

    peacefully. _____

4. Chickadees sing "Chickadeedeedee!" _____

5. Blue Jays have big appetites, and they often screech.

    _____

6. Nuthatches do acrobatic tricks, so people call them upside-down birds.

    _____

7. Mourning doves make soft cooing sounds whenever they perch in trees.

    _____

Here are some simple sentences that Barry wrote. Edit each pair to form a compound sentence. Use conjunctions from the word bank.

> **Conjunctions**
>
> and    or    but    so    nor

8. My favorite bird is the chickadee. _____ My brother likes cardinals.

9. Mourning doves don't like the bird feeder. _____ They eat seeds on the ground.

10. Evening grosbeaks have bad tempers. _____ Sometimes they fight.

11. Suet attracts woodpeckers. _____ I keep that feeder full.

12. Most birds love sunflower seeds. _____ They like cracked corn, too.

13. Hummingbirds do not eat seeds. _____ They do not eat corn.

Write complex sentences using these dependent clauses. For each, add a related idea that is complete and can stand alone.

14. Whenever it snows, _____

15. If I could fly, _____

16. After winter ends, _____

17. Before she ate, _____

18. When birds sing, _____

**Editing**   Edit Barry's journal entry so it can be printed in the school newspaper. Make it flow smoothly by creating compound or complex sentences.

| Mistakes | |
| --- | --- |
| Spelling | 5 |

I like feeding wild birds. I like waching wild birds. Many different and colorful birds come to my feeder. Goldfinches squabble and argue. Evening grosbeaks argu too. Both tipes of birds are black and yellow. Goldfinches are small birds. Evening grosbeaks are much larger. Sometimes gray squirrels clime into the feeder. They love to feest on fat sunflower seeds. Then the blue jays gang up. The blue jays try to scare the squirrels away.

# FRAGMENTS, RUN-ONS, COMMA SPLICES

## Become a Super Writer

Jan is writing a report on the history of the bicycle. On the left is what she wrote first. On the right are her revised sentences.

| | |
|---|---|
| (1) Invented around 1790. | It was invented around 1790. |
| (2) Riders pushed the walk-along with their feet it was like a kiddie car a new model appeared in 1810. | Riders pushed the walk-along with their feet. It was like a kiddie car. A new model appeared in 1810. |
| (3) An inventor attached a steering bar to the front wheel in 1816, pedals were added in 1860. | An inventor attached a steering bar to the front wheel in 1816. Pedals were added in 1860. |

The first thing Jan wrote is a sentence **fragment**. The next is a **run-on**; it has three different ideas all run together. Last, Jan "spliced" two sentences together with a comma. This error is called a **comma splice**.

## Definitions · Usage

A **fragment** is an incomplete thought.
A **run-on** is two or more complete sentences joined without either punctuation or a conjunction.
A **comma splice** has two sentences joined by a comma but with no conjunction.

## Your Turn

Write *F* to identify fragments, *RO* for run-ons, or *CS* for comma splices.

_____ 1. Walk-along bicycles were also called hobby horses, a French inventor patented a bicycle called the Boneshaker in 1866.

_____ 2. The high-wheeler was invented in England the front wheel was nearly as tall as a person the back wheel was small.

_____ 3. Rode the high-wheeler.

_____ 4. The bicycle we know was first made in 1880, both wheels were the same size.

_____ 5. Improvements like rubber tires, brakes, and gears.

_____ 6. Cycling is very popular today it is fun it's good exercise.

**Revise these comma splices. Add a conjunction to each that makes sense.**

7. Both cyclists and motorists must follow traffic regulations, _____ they must yield to pedestrians.

8. Helmets and correct hand signals help keep cyclists safe, _____ taking good care of a bike is important for safety.

9. There are bicycle safety programs in many cities, _____ many parents enroll their children.

10. Riding on a bike's handlebars is dangerous, _____ unless your bike is built for two, ride by yourself at all times.

**Write a complete sentence using each of these fragments.**

11. Riding more than two abreast.

_____

12. Suddenly the traffic light.

_____

13. Joshua's new ten-speed bike.

_____

14. A tandem bike, or a bike for two.

_____

15. Today most young riders.

_____

**Editing**  **Apply your editing brakes to this paragraph. It is one long run-on sentence. Use punctuation to break it up.**

| Mistakes | | |
|---|---|---|
| | Capitalization | 4 |
| | Punctuation | 6 |
| | Spelling | 4 |

Always signal stops and turns with you left arm so motorists and pedestrians know what you plan to do wach out for cars parking or leeving the curb sumtimes drivers pay so much attention to traffic that they dont see a cyclist approaching it is safer to walk your bike across busy intersections than to ride it across them be sure to wear clothes that won't get caught in the bike's gears or chain.

_____

# COMBINING AND EXPANDING SENTENCES

## Become a Super Writer

Ed and his dad built a bookcase. Later, Ed wrote about the experience.

*Dad measured the wall. We bought lumber. We got home. We unloaded the lumber. I fetched Dad's tools. He showed me how to read the tape measure. I measured the boards.*

When Ed reread his writing, he realized that it needed revision.

*Dad measured the wall, and we bought lumber at the building supply store. When we got home, we unloaded the lumber. I fetched Dad's hammer, power saw, and tape measure. He showed me how to read the tape measure. Then I carefully measured the boards.*

Notice how Ed joined simple sentences to form compound or complex sentences. He also added details to make the sentences more interesting.

### Rules

> Two or more simple sentences can be **combined** to form a compound subject or predicate, a compound sentence, or a complex sentence. Details can be added to **expand** any kind of sentence to make it more interesting.

## Your Turn

**Combine each pair of sentences.**

1. I carefully measured each board. I cut each board.

   _____

2. The power saw whined loudly. It spat sawdust on the floor.

   _____

3. I hammered the nails slowly. I didn't want to pound my thumb.

   _____

4. Dad and I put on protective goggles. Dad used the power saw.

   _____

5. The sawdust smelled good. It tickled my nose.

   _____

6. Dad let me use a hand saw. Sawing by hand is hard work.

   _____

While he was sanding the bookcase, Ed got a splinter. Help Ed describe what happened. Use phrases and clauses from the word bank and ideas of your own to expand the sentences.

| | | |
|---|---|---|
| it was easy until | sticking out of my finger | because it was so tiny |
| by using tweezers | after getting the splinter | so Dad rescued me |
| when it happened | when working with wood | |

7. My hand slipped. _____
_____

8. It surprised me. _____
_____

9. It was nearly invisible. _____
_____

10. Dad pulled it out. _____
_____

11. The splinter hurt my finger. _____
_____

12. Dad warned me. _____
_____

13. I sanded carefully. _____
_____

 **Editing** Read more about Ed's carpentry experiences. Find and edit the sentences he can combine. Expand other sentences by adding details.

| Mistakes | |
|---|---|
| Spelling | 4 |

One bored was too short. I made a misteak measuring it. I thought Dad would skold me. He didn't. He said, "Every carpentor makes mistakes, Ed." I hurried. That's what caused the mistake. Next time, I slowed down. I took my time measuring. Dad checked my work. He smiled. He sawed the board. He said I did a good job. I felt proud. Dad handed me the hammer. He handed me some nails. He held the boards together. I nailed them.

# KINDS OF SENTENCES

## Become a Super Writer

Kim is working on a how-to article. She decided it would be fun to write about something different—like making sun ice tea. Here's her introduction.

| | |
|---|---|
| My favorite summer drink is sun ice tea. | declarative |
| Is it difficult to make this kind of tea? | interrogative |
| Not at all! | exclamatory |
| Try this recipe. See for yourself how easy it is. | imperative |

Kim wanted to make her introduction interesting. Notice that she used four different **kinds of sentences**. Variety adds "spice" to one's writing.

### Definitions·Usage

A **declarative** sentence makes a statement. It ends with a period.
An **interrogative** sentence asks a question. It ends with a question mark.
An **exclamatory** sentence shows surprise or strong feeling. It ends with an exclamation point.
An **imperative** sentence gives a command or makes a request. It ends with a period. *You* is understood, even though it is not stated.

## Your Turn

**Label each type of sentence. Write** *Declarative, Imperative, Interrogative,* **or** *Exclamatory.* **Add the correct punctuation to each sentence.**

1. What kind of tea should you use    _____

2. I prefer herbal or decaffeinated teas    _____

3. Put eight teabags in a pitcher    _____

4. Do NOT let the tea-bag tags fall in    _____

5. Fill the pitcher with cold water    _____

6. You need to set the pitcher in the sun    _____

7. The sunshine will brew the tea    _____

8. Wow, that tastes great    _____

9. Would you like some lemon    _____

**Writing her how-to article got Kim interested in tea. She did some research and found these facts. Rewrite Kim's sentences so that they're not all declarative.**

10. Tea is an ancient beverage.

_____

11. People drank tea in China as early as the 500s.

_____

12. Europeans learned about tea in the 1700s.

_____

13. Dutch traders brought back tea leaves from China.

_____

14. Black, green, and oolong tea are now very popular.

_____

15. There's a legend about how tea came into use.

_____

16. A holy person in India felt sleepy.

_____

17. He chewed on some tea leaves and suddenly was awake.

_____

18. That's why people drink decaffeinated tea.

_____

 **Editing**  **Edit Kim's sentences. Add the correct punctuation and capitalization.**

| Mistakes | | |
|---|---|---|
| | Capitalization | 6 |
| | Punctuation | 8 |
| | Spelling | 6 |

Tea plants grow in India, China, Sri Lanka, Japan, and Indonesia wild tea plants

grow to a hieght of thiry feet or more Cultivated tea plants are actually small

shrubs They are pruned to the height of a person or even shorter pruning forses

the shrub to produce more leafs can you imagine what a tea leaf looks like it is

long and leathery, much like the leaf of a willow tree once a year the tea plant

blosoms the flowers are ever so luvely

# COMMON AND PROPER NOUNS

## Become a Super Writer

Sam is writing a report about our national anthem. Read his first sentence.

An <u>anthem</u> is a <u>song</u> of <u>praise</u> or of <u>patriotism</u>.

The underlined words are all **common nouns**. Here's the next sentence in Sam's report.

Our national anthem is "<u>The Star-Spangled Banner</u>," which was written by <u>Francis Scott Key</u>.

Notice that the man's name and the name of the anthem are capitalized. These are **proper nouns**.

### Definitions · Usage

A **common noun** is the general name of a person, place, thing, or idea.
A **proper noun** is the specific name for a person, place, or thing. Capitalize the important words in a proper noun.

## Your Turn

**Read Sam's report on "The Star-Spangled Banner." Underline the common nouns and capitalize the proper nouns.**

1. francis scott key worked as a lawyer in washington, d.c.

2. He achieved fame when he wrote "the star-spangled banner."

3. key wrote the words for the song during the war of 1812.

4. The british were bombarding fort mchenry in baltimore.

5. At that time, key was on a boat in chesapeake bay.

6. Throughout the night, he watched the attack.

7. Despite a terrible battle, the flag was still there in the morning.

8. key was so inspired, he created a poem on the spot.

9. He wrote the words on the back of an unfinished letter.

10. He used the tune of the English song "to anacreon in heaven."

**Write eight sentences on the lines below. Use common nouns and proper nouns from the word bank. Be sure to capitalize the proper nouns.**

| Common Nouns | Proper Nouns |
|---|---|
| anthem | washington |
| battle | congress |
| lawyer | "the star-spangled banner" |
| poem | war of 1812 |
| ship | chesapeake bay |
| words | september 1814 |
| tune | francis scott key |
| flag | america |
| letter | english |
| song | fort mchenry |

11. _____

12. _____

13. _____

14. _____

15. _____

16. _____

17. _____

18. _____

 **Editing** Read this paragraph from Sam's report. Capitalize all the proper nouns. Correct the misspelled common nouns.

| Mistakes | |
|---|---|
| Capitalization | 22 |
| Spelling | 3 |

Key was born on august 1, 1779, in maryland. He went to st. johns college in

annapolis, maryland. In 1801 he got a job in a law ofice. key became district

attorney of the district of columbia in 1833. Two years later, President andrew

jackson asked him to settle a dispyute with the creek indians in alabama. key was

never serious about his poetry, though he wrote enough pomes to fill a collection.

He called it "poems of the late francis s. key, esq."

# Singular and Plural Nouns

## Become a Super Writer

Janine is interested in mythology. She is writing a report on myths. Here is her first sentence.

A <u>myth</u> is a <u>story</u> that explains <u>something</u> in <u>nature.</u>

The four underlined words are nouns. Each noun is singular. Now read Janine's second sentence.

<u>People</u> ask why <u>things</u> like <u>echoes</u> and <u>mountains</u> exist.

The underlined nouns in this sentence are all **plural**. Notice that most plural nouns—but not all—end with *s*.

**Definitions**

A **singular noun** names one person, place, thing, or idea.
A **plural noun** names more than one person, place, thing, or idea.
Many plural nouns are formed by adding *s* or *es* to the singular form.

## Your Turn

**Read more of Janine's report. Underline the singular nouns. Circle the plural nouns.**

1. We know things about our world that those living long ago didn't.
2. Scientists have given us explanations for many natural events.
3. The ancient Greeks made up a wonderful story to explain echoes.
4. The tale told of a handsome young man and a nymph named Echo.
5. Echo loved the youth, but he treated her with coldness.
6. Echo was so hurt that she faded away to nothing but her voice.
7. Today we know that echoes are not the voices of sad nymphs.
8. When we shout, sound waves travel through the air in all directions.
9. If the waves hit a large object, they may bounce back and reach our ears a second time.
10. In valleys and canyons, sound waves bounce from wall to wall and produce several echoes.

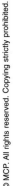

**Write the missing singular or plural nouns in the word bank below.**

| Singular | Plural | Singular | Plural |
|----------|--------|----------|--------|
| tail → _____ | | fox → _____ | |
| _____ → bears | | _____ → trees | |
| squirrel → _____ | | hole → _____ | |

**Use the words in the word bank to finish the myth about why Bear has a short tail.**

Once upon a time, Bear had the longest, most beautiful tail in the world. All the other animals were jealous of Bear's tail. One day _____

_____

_____

_____

_____

_____

_____

 **Editing** — **Read the end of Janine's report. Correct the plural nouns that she misspelled.**

| Mistakes | |
|----------|---|
| Punctuation | 2 |
| Spelling | 6 |

In time, these kindes of stories were told about almost every object in nature The rustling of leaves meant the goddess who lived in the tree spoke in a murmuring voice. The hurrying stream was a nymph rushing to join her friend, the sea The starrs were good people whom the gods placed in the sky so that everyone remembered their good deedes. Even though we now have scientific explanationes for such thing, these mythes are still wonderful stories to read and to retell.

# IRREGULAR PLURAL NOUNS

## Become a Super Writer

While Miles was visiting his grandparents, he wrote a letter to a classmate. Here's a sentence from his letter.

*Grandma showed me the flock of sheep.*

Flocks have many sheep, so Miles saw numerous sheep. *Sheep* is an **irregular plural noun**.

**Definition**

An **irregular plural noun** does not end in *s* or *es*. In the word bank are some common irregular plural nouns.

| SINGULAR | PLURAL | SINGULAR | PLURAL | SINGULAR | PLURAL |
|----------|--------|----------|----------|----------|--------|
| sheep | sheep | deer | deer | moose | moose |
| foot | feet | child | children | mouse | mice |
| louse | lice | ox | oxen | goose | geese |
| tooth | teeth | woman | women | man | men |

## Your Turn

**Read each sentence. Write *S* for singular or *P* for plural to tell if each underlined noun is singular or plural. Circle the clue word or words that helped you decide.**

_____ 1. Several <u>deer</u> ate the apples in the backyard.

_____ 2. The apple trees are only thirty <u>feet</u> from the farmhouse.

_____ 3. Grandma's parlor rang with the voices of happy <u>children</u>.

_____ 4. The cat caught a <u>mouse</u> in the cellar.

_____ 5. When my cousin fell from the loft, he chipped two <u>teeth</u>.

_____ 6. I saw a huge <u>moose</u> swimming in the lake.

_____ 7. Do you know the <u>man</u> who is going to buy Grandpa's old car?

_____ 8. Shearing the herd of <u>sheep</u> on the neighbor's farm keeps everyone busy.

_____ 9. Before there were tractors, farmers often used a pair of <u>oxen</u> to plow their fields.

**Read each sentence. Circle the irregular plural noun. Write its singular form in the puzzle.**

**Across**

2. A vet came to look at the horse's feet.

4. A herd of moose drank from our stream.

6. We chased away some men who wanted to hunt.

7. Our sheep are easily frightened by loud noise.

8. The old horse blanket was filled with lice.

9. We saw deer in that meadow.

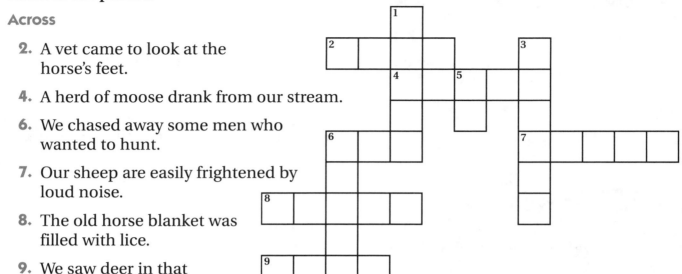

**Down**

1. Several women got together to make a quilt.

3. People here like the look of a handmade quilt.

5. The old yolk used for oxen is now an antique.

6. Our cat loves to chase mice out of the barn.

 **Editing**   **Read more of Miles's letter. Correct the plural nouns that he misspelled.**

| Mistakes | | |
|---|---|---|
| | Capitalization | 2 |
| | Punctuation | 3 |
| | Spelling | 4 |

Taking care of animals is a full-time job on a farm. Lambs are born in the spring. Before long they are full-grown sheeps? shearing them is a big job I couldn't believe how one men was able to hold the sheep down and shear it at the same time. Calfs are born in the spring too. They are so funny when they try to stand. They wobble! did you know that baby gooses are called goslings. By the way, if the plural of *goose* is *geese*, how come the plural of *moose* isn't *meese*?

# POSSESSIVE NOUNS

## Become a Super Writer

Mary wrote these sentences in a biography of Pocahontas.

Pocahontas was <u>Powhatan's</u> daughter.

The <u>settlers'</u> lives depended on the good will of the Native Americans.

*Powhatan's* is a **singular possessive noun**. *Settlers'* is a **plural possessive noun**.

---

**Definition · Usage**

A **possessive noun** shows possession or ownership.

- Add *'s* to form the possessive of a singular noun.
- Add just an apostrophe to form the possessive of a plural noun that already ends in *s*. If a plural noun does not end in *s*, ad *'s*.

---

## Your Turn

**Read these sentences from Mary's biography. On each line, write the correct possessive form of the noun in parentheses.**

1. Captain John Smith was the English _____ leader. (colonists)

2. Pocahontas is supposed to have saved the _____ life. (man)

3. _____ book, *True Relation of Virginia,* says that Powhatan wanted to kill Smith. (Smith)

4. Pocahontas begged for her _____ mercy, and Smith's life was spared. (father)

5. Some historians don't think the _____ story is true. (author)

6. In 1614, _____ marriage to an English settler took place. (Pocahontas)

7. Her _____ name was John Rolfe. (husband)

8. The _____ travels took them to England. (couple)

9. When Pocahontas died of smallpox, the British mourned the _____ death. (princess)

10. Her son Thomas later became one of _____ important citizens. (Virginia)

**Write five sentences of your own about Pocahontas or the Jamestown settlers. Use nouns from the word bank. Include a possessive noun in each sentence.**

> Native Americans    settlers    father    daughter    husband
>
> wife    Englishmen    colonists    people    princess    Thomas

11. _____

_____

12. _____

_____

13. _____

_____

14. _____

_____

15. _____

_____

**Editing**    Read more about Powhatan and his people in Mary's biography. Correct the mistakes in the underlined possessive nouns.

| Mistakes | |
| --- | --- |
| Punctuation | 7 |
| Spelling | 5 |

   Powhatans' tribe controlled the Powhatan Confederacy of Virginia. This confederacy onse included 30 different tribes. The English made their first settlment among the Native Americans'. Powhatan was at first freindly toward the English. He sent food when the settler's crops failed. However, the colonist's demands finally made him angry. Fighting between the two groops ended in 1614, when Pocahontas became John Rolfes' wive. Pocahontas' father then helped the settlers until his death in 1618. The leaders' real name was Wahunsonacock, but he called himself Powhatan after his favorite village.

# SENTENCES AND NOUNS

**Tell whether each sentence is simple, compound, or complex.**

1. Harriet Tubman escaped from slavery before the Civil War.
   _____

2. Tubman led other slaves to freedom, which was often very risky for her. _____

3. During the war she worked as a nurse, but she also spied for the Union. _____

**Correct these fragments, run-ons, and comma splices.**

4. As a girl Harriet Tubman.

   _____

5. She escaped in 1849, she traveled north to Pennsylvania.

   _____

6. Congress passed the Fugitive Slave Law in 1850 and slave owners followed runaways into free states and many slaves fled to Canada.

   _____

   _____

**Combine these sentences.**

7. The Underground Railroad was not a railroad. It was not under the ground, either.

   _____

**Expand the sentence.**

8. Southern slaves helped runaways.

   _____

**Write *declarative, interrogative, exclamatory,* or *imperative* to tell what kind of sentence each is.**

9. Martin is writing a report about Harriet Tubman. _____

10. Did you finish your research yet, Martin? _____

11. Read this article about the Underground Railroad. _____

12. What a brave woman Harriet Tubman was! _____

**Circle the common nouns and underline the proper nouns in these sentences.**

13. More Americans died in the Civil War than in any other war in history.

14. Gary and Pauline are writing a report on the Battle of Gettysburg.

15. Gary visited the battlefield in Pennsylvania with his family.

16. General Robert E. Lee led the Confederate army during the battle.

17. The leader of the Union army was General George C. Meade.

**Choose the noun in each set of parentheses that correctly completes the sentence.**

18. One of the (wars, war's) bloodiest battles was the Battle of Gettysburg, which took place in 1863 and lasted three (day, days).

19. Most (people, person) consider the Battle of Gettysburg a very important point in the (war, war's).

20. The Confederate (army, armies) had about 75,000 (soldier, soldiers).

21. General Meade led a (group, groups) of about 90,000 (troop, troops).

22. The two (armys, armies) met accidentally at Gettysburg while the Confederates were looking for (shoe, shoes).

23. On July 3, 1863, (Lees', Lee's) soldiers returned to Virginia, but (Meade's, Meades) troops did not follow him.

24. Lee lost more than 20,000 (mans, men), while Meade had about 18,000 (loss's, losses).

25. (Lincoln's, Lincolns) Gettysburg Address was given on the battlefield five (monthes, months) later.

**Complete each sentence with the plural form of a word in the word bank. Use each word only once.**

26. During the war, both the North and the South had _____ .

27. Many brave _____ fought in the battles.

28. Some, such as bugle boys, were only _____ .

29. Six hundred thousand Americans lost their _____ in the war.

30. Although most _____ didn't fight, they helped in other ways.

> hero
> man
> woman
> life
> child

# SENTENCES AND NOUNS

**Choose the best label for each group of words below. Fill in the circle by your answer.**

1. Little or no rain falls in the desert.
   - ○ simple sentence
   - ○ compound sentence
   - ○ complex sentence
   - ○ fragment
   - ○ run-on
   - ○ comma splice

2. Fewer than 10 inches of rain.
   - ○ simple sentence
   - ○ compound sentence
   - ○ complex sentence
   - ○ fragment
   - ○ run-on
   - ○ comma splice

3. Since plants need water, few plants grow in the desert.
   - ○ simple sentence
   - ○ compound sentence
   - ○ complex sentence
   - ○ fragment
   - ○ run-on
   - ○ comma splice

4. The cactus stores a lot of water, and its roots absorb water quickly.
   - ○ simple sentence
   - ○ compound sentence
   - ○ complex sentence
   - ○ fragment
   - ○ run-on
   - ○ comma splice

5. Some cactuses are small, others like the saguaro are huge.
   - ○ simple sentence
   - ○ compound sentence
   - ○ complex sentence
   - ○ fragment
   - ○ run-on
   - ○ comma splice

6. The saguaro cactus is woody the Native Americans used them for fuel they built their homes from them.
   - ○ simple sentence
   - ○ compound sentence
   - ○ complex sentence
   - ○ fragment
   - ○ run-on
   - ○ comma splice

**Fill in the circle by the answer that tells what kind of sentence each one is.**

7. Can animals live in the desert?   ○ interrogative   ○ exclamatory

8. Small animals live below the surface, where it is cooler.   ○ declarative   ○ imperative

9. What an interesting fact!   ○ exclamatory   ○ imperative

10. Always carry water with you in the desert.   ○ interrogative   ○ imperative

**Read the sentences. Choose the sentence below the pair that shows how the sentences can be combined.**

11. Sharp spines protect most cactuses. Animals avoid the spines.

    ○ Sharp spines protect most cactuses. Animals avoid them.

    ○ Sharp spines protect most cactuses, and animals avoid the spines.

**Read the sentence. Choose the sentence below it that shows how the sentence can be expanded.**

12. One kind of cactus blooms at midnight.

    ○ One kind of cactus blooms when the desert cools.

    ○ One kind of cactus, the cereus, blooms at midnight when the desert cools.

**Identify the kind of noun underlined in each sentence. Fill in the circle by your answer.**

13. Mule <u>deer</u> are large desert animals.

    ○ singular common noun          ○ singular possessive noun

    ○ proper noun                   ○ irregular plural noun

14. The dingo lives in the deserts of <u>Australia</u>.

    ○ plural common noun            ○ plural possessive noun

    ○ proper noun                   ○ irregular plural noun

15. A <u>camel's</u> humps are used to store food.

    ○ singular common noun          ○ singular possessive noun

    ○ plural common noun            ○ plural possessive noun

16. Kangaroo rats get water from the <u>plants</u> they eat.

    ○ plural common noun            ○ plural possessive noun

    ○ proper noun                   ○ irregular plural noun

17. <u>Animals'</u> different qualities help them to survive in the desert.

    ○ singular common noun          ○ singular possessive noun

    ○ plural common noun            ○ plural possessive noun

NAME _____

# ACTION VERBS

## Become a Super Writer

Jack wrote a play for his class. He included these stage directions.

Jessica <u>moves</u> toward the door at stage right.

When Jack revised the directions, he replaced the word *moves* with *dashes*.

Jessica <u>dashes</u> toward the door at stage right.

*Dashes* tells what Jessica does. *Dashes* shows the **action** more clearly. It tells specifically how Jessica moves. Jack could also have changed the word *moves* to a word such as *skips, glides,* or *shuffles.*

Jessica <u>shuffles</u> to the door at stage right.

*Shuffles* tells specifically how Jessica moves.

**Definition · Usage**

An **action verb** tells what the subject does. Use action verbs to make your writing clear and specific.

## Your Turn

**Read Jack's research about play production. Underline the action verb in each sentence.**

1. A playwright writes the script for a play.

2. The actors recite the lines on stage.

3. Each actor plays a different role, such as hero or villain.

4. The director guides all the actors.

5. Theater carpenters build the sets, or scenery.

6. The stage crew places the sets in the right positions.

7. Lighting technicians shine the lights on sets and actors.

8. Makeup artists apply makeup to the actors.

9. Seamstresses sew the wardrobe.

10. The publicity staff advertises the play to the public.

11. The sales staff sells the tickets for the play.

12. Ushers distribute programs to the audience.

Circle the action verb in each sentence. Choose another verb from the word bank that shows the action more clearly. Write the new action verb on the line. Be sure the verb agrees with the subject.

| ring | run | scream | rush into | shout |
|------|-----|--------|-----------|-------|
| exclaim | hug | burst into | race | jump |
| shriek | dance | smile | sing | race |

13. On stage, a telephone sounds three times. _____

14. A young girl goes quickly to the phone. _____

15. Surprised by the message, she calls, "Mom!" _____

16. Her mother enters the room in a hurry. _____

17. The fearful mother says, "What's wrong?" _____

18. The girl says, "I'm the contest winner!" _____

19. The girl moves toward her mother. _____

20. They hold each other. _____

21. Together they move around the stage. _____

22. They look at each other happily. _____

**Editing** Underline the action verbs in Jack's E-mail message. Then replace some of these verbs with more specific action verbs. Reread the paragraph to be sure it makes sense.

| Mistakes | |
|----------|---|
| Spelling | 5 |

We practiced this play for many weeks. You know your lines. You must also show your feelings with your actions and voice. Acters look at different people for ideas for characters. An actor uses his body to express emostion. He hits his fist on a tabel to show anger. He crys to show sorrow. For a frightened character, the actor steps back. A confident character walks across the stage. A shy character stays in the background. A good actor changes his voice for different characters. Strong characters speak loudly. Weak characters speak softly. Some characters do not speak at al.

# MAIN AND HELPING VERBS

## Become a Super Writer

Margo spent several hours at the computer last night. Here is the note she wrote to her mother before going to bed.

Dear Mom,

I (have) turned the computer off, as promised. I (was) working on the Internet until 10 p.m. I (have) not had time to print out all my research. I (will) need this information when I write my report. (Can) you keep Timmy away from the computer today, please?

Love,
Margo

Each underlined verb phrase has a **main verb** and a **helping verb**. The helping verb is circled.

**Definitions**

> The **main verb** tells what the subject does. The **helping verb** helps the main verb state an action or show time.

### HELPING VERBS

| | | |
|---|---|---|
| am | does | is |
| are | had | shall |
| can | has | was |
| do | have | will |

## Your Turn

**Here are sentences from Margo's report. Underline the main verbs and circle the helping verbs.**

1. Nowadays on TV, advertising is running the show.

2. Some shows are devoting eight minutes out of every thirty to commercials.

3. Some commercials can appear more than once during a TV program.

4. Are you persuaded by advertising?

5. Some advertisements can frighten people into a purchase.

6. Other commercials will win us over with humor.

7. Sports celebrities have sold many products.

8. Public service ads have encouraged good health habits.

9. This kind of advertising has helped fight disease.

10. Have commercials influenced you?

11. I shall watch TV more carefully in the future.

DRINK MILK

**Circle the main verb in each sentence. Think of a helping verb to use with that main verb. Rewrite the sentence, using the helping verb. Change the form of the main verb, if necessary.**

**12.** Advertisers learn a lot about people.

_____

**13.** They research buyers' habits.

_____

**14.** Manufacturers test products on groups of people.

_____

**15.** Some advertisers discover the best colors for packaging.

_____

**16.** Advertisers match commercials to the audience.

_____

**17.** Public television receives little or no money from advertising.

_____

**18.** Public television relies on donations.

_____

 **Editing** Margo's mom wrote her a note. Find and correct three mistakes in the use of helping verbs.

| Mistakes | |
|---|---|
| Spelling | 5 |

Dear Margo,

I was sorry when I saw your note, because I are hoping that you had printed your reserch. Timmy has been nawty today. He is only five years old. He thinks he is old enuff to help, so he have tried to help you with your report. He turned on the computer, and deleted your infomation. I can help you recover some of your work tonight. In the meantime, I have look for some articles at the libary.

Love,

Mom

# LINKING VERBS

## Become a Super Writer

Henry visited Bryce National Park with his family. Here are some entries from his journal.

Bryce <u>is</u> a famous (park) in Utah.

The rock formations there <u>look</u> (fantastic.)

In the first sentence, the **linking verb** *is* connects the noun *park* with the subject *Bryce*. In the second sentence, the linking verb *look* connects the adjective *fantastic* with the subject *formations*.

> **Definition · Usage**
>
> A **linking verb** connects the subject of a sentence with a noun or an adjective in the predicate. It tells what the subject is or is like.

**LINKING VERBS**

| | |
|---|---|
| be | appear |
| look | taste |
| feel | seem |

## Your Turn

**Henry researched other national parks. Underline the linking verb in each sentence. Draw an arrow to connect the noun or the adjective in the predicate with the subject.**

1. Denali National Park in Alaska is still mostly wild.

2. Grand Canyon National Park is 227 miles long.

3. Visitors are "astronauts for a day" at the Space and Rocket Center in Alabama.

4. The coast of Acadia National Park in Bar Harbor, Maine, is young.

5. The animals in the San Diego Zoo seem content in the park.

6. Tourists look like sailors in photos taken at Mystic Seaport in Connecticut.

7. Americans feel proud at Kennedy Space Center in Florida.

8. The Children's Museum in Indianapolis is an adventure for curious kids.

9. The shapes of the saguaro cactuses in the Sonoran Desert seem almost human.

10. The village of Williamsburg, Virginia, appears as it did in the 1700s.

11. The wood in the Petrified Forest feels as hard as a rock.

**Help Henry share the following information with his classmates. Complete each sentence with a linking verb.**

12. An early passenger car at the B&O Museum in Maryland _____ a double-decker stagecoach on wheels.

13. Computer history _____ an attraction at Boston's Computer Museum.

14. Meramec Caverns in Missouri _____ a hideout for the outlaw Jesse James.

15. The Hoover Dam _____ one of the modern wonders of the world.

16. Time _____ forgotten at the Harold Warp Pioneer Village in Nebraska.

17. The one-room schoolhouse _____ the same today as it did in 1935.

18. Visitors _____ amazed at the inventions displayed at the Edison National Historic Site in New Jersey.

19. Niagara Falls _____ a tempting challenge to high-wire daredevils.

20. Annie Taylor _____ the first person to go over the falls in a barrel— and live to tell about it.

21. A baseball at the National Baseball Hall of Fame at Cooperstown _____ 100 years old.

22. Now you _____ an expert on national parks!

**Editing** Here is a paragraph from a report Henry wrote. Underline the linking verb in each sentence.

| Mistakes | |
|---|---|
| Capitalization | 2 |
| Punctuation | 2 |
| Spelling | 4 |

Many national parks are interesting. I am excited by their many different themes. But my dream is a trip to a sumer camp called Future Astronaut Training Program. The camp's location is the Kansas Cosmosphere & Space Center? Only students in seventh, eighth, and ninth grades are eligible. campers wear space soots and eat space food They also are waitless. the big finish is a launch and landing of a simulated shuttle flite. Maybe one day I will even be a real astronaut. Dreams are fun to think about. I can be anything in a dream. Are you a dreamer?

# VERB TENSES: PRESENT, PAST, FUTURE

## Become a Super Writer

Whitney is writing a report on the history of toys. Here is her first paragraph.

> Long ago, children <u>played</u> with rocks and animal bones. Today children play electronic games on computers. In the future, they <u>will play</u> with games that haven't been designed yet.

Whitney wanted to begin by telling about the **past**, **present**, and **future** of toys. Notice that she used a form of the verb *play* in each sentence. *Played* tells about an action that happened in the past. *Play* tells about a present action. *Will play* describes a future action. Whitney used three different **tenses** of the verb *play*.

**Definition**

> **Verb tense** tells when the action of a verb takes place. Three common tenses are **past**, **present**, and **future**.

## Your Turn

**Underline the verb or verb phrase in each sentence.
Show the verb's tense by writing *past*, *present*, or *future*.**

1. Morris Michtom created the first teddy bear in 1906. _____

2. Michtom named his toy in honor of President Theodore Roosevelt. _____

3. The President's family and close friends called him "Teddy." _____

4. The toymaker noticed a cartoon of Teddy Roosevelt with a bear. _____

5. He asked the President's permission to use his name. _____

6. Some people collect teddy bears as a hobby. _____

7. People will always love these huggable stuffed animals. _____

8. In 1959, Barbie Handlin liked teenage dolls better than baby dolls. _____

9. Working in the garage, Barbie's parents made a teenage doll. _____

10. You will probably guess the doll's name in a second—Barbie! _____

11. Do you know the history of any other toys? _____

**Write a verb to complete each sentence. Use the past, present, or future tense of the verb in parentheses.**

**12.** Many years ago, Joshua Lionel Cowen _____ Lionel trains. (invent)

**13.** Lionel trains _____ like real-life trains, but are much, much smaller. (look)

**14.** Cowen first _____ a model flatcar with a motor. (produce)

**15.** In the 1930s he _____ a whistle to some of his locomotives. (add)

**16.** In the 1940s, smoke _____ from some of his steam locomotives. (billow)

**17.** Today a set of electric trains _____ locomotives, boxcars, cabooses, and even train stations. (include)

**18.** People have often _____ tiny villages to go with their train sets. (create)

**19.** Some people have _____ whole cities for their train layout. (design)

**20.** The trains themselves _____ in different sizes, or scales, such as HO, O, N, S, Z, and G. (come)

**21.** For years to come, many children _____ Lionel trains as gifts. (receive)

**Editing** — Read Whitney's paragraph about the history of another toy. Correct six mistakes in the use of verb tenses.

| Mistakes | |
|---|---|
| Spelling | 3 |

The Danish carpenter Godtfred Kirk-Christiansen liked his job as a toymaker. He turn small bilding blocks into toys. One day a shopkeeper complain. "I see no purpus in these toys," he said. Godtfred agree. He created a new kind of block. The new blocks lock onto one another. Godtfred call his toy Legos. The word *Lego* in Danish means "play well." His new blocks become very populer. Many children have "played well" with their Legos.

# PRINCIPAL PARTS AND PARTICIPLES

## Become a Super Writer

Carly kept a journal during her visit to an animal theme park. Read these sentences from her journal.

*The gates usually open at seven a.m. Today the park is opening on time. Mom awakened me at five. She has never awakened me that early!*

The verbs in Carly's sentences are underlined.

### Definitions · Usage

A verb has four basic forms, or **principal parts**.
The **present** is the basic form.
The **present participle** ends with *ing* and is used with a form of *be*.
The **past** ends with *ed*.
The **past participle** ends with *ed* and is used with *have, has,* or *had*.

### PRINCIPAL PARTS OF REGULAR VERBS

| Present | Present Participle | Past | Past Participle |
|---------|--------------------|------|------------------|
| open | (is) opening | opened | (has) opened |
| awaken | (is) awakening | awakened | (has) awakened |

## Your Turn

Read these sentences. For each underlined verb or verb phrase, tell which principal part is used. Write *A* for present, *B* for present participle, *C* for past, or *D* for past participle.

1. We <u>arrived</u> at the theme park early in the day. _____

2. The main gates of the park <u>were</u> just <u>opening</u>. _____

3. We <u>headed</u> immediately for the African safari. _____

4. A line of people <u>had</u> already <u>formed</u> there. _____

5. Before long, we <u>hopped</u> onto our safari vehicle. _____

6. We <u>were skidding</u> along over bumpy trails,
   on the lookout for animals. _____

7. We <u>bounced</u> over a rickety bridge with
   crocodiles below. _____

8. This <u>is</u> one amazing adventure! _____

When Carly returned to school, her friends asked lots of questions. Write complete sentences that tell what you think her answers were. Underline the principal parts of your verbs.

**9.** Was the elephant roaming on the savanna?

_____

**10.** Had the baby elephant followed her mother into the brush?

_____

**11.** Was the rickety old bridge really collapsing?

_____

**12.** Were the crocodiles smiling up at you?

_____

**13.** What other animals did you see?

_____

**14.** Had you ever visited a savanna before?

_____

**15.** Was the road really flooded out in some places?

_____

**16.** Did you enjoy your trip to the theme park?

_____

 **Editing** Edit this paragraph of Carly's report. Find and correct four mistakes in the principal parts of verbs.

| Mistakes | |
|---|---|
| Capitalization | 3 |
| Punctuation | 3 |

After the safari, we visited the Conservation Station. I was learned a lot about animals there. a guide was showed us a baby hedgehog. Spines cover a hedgehog's back Short fur grows on the underside of its body, a scared hedgehog is rolled itself into a ball. The hedgehog hunts for food at night. it sleeps all winter. Some people liking them as pets. I am hoping to get one?

NAME _____

# IRREGULAR VERBS, PART 1

## Become a Super Writer

Mina was writing about life in the American colonies in 1776. She wrote:

Most colonists maked their living by farming.

*Maked* didn't sound right to Mina. She remembered that *make* is an **irregular verb**. The past of *make* is *made*. Mina changed her sentence.

**Usage**

The principal parts of **irregular verbs** are formed in special ways. Some have the same past and past participle, and others have the same present and past participle.

## PRINCIPAL PARTS OF IRREGULAR VERBS

### Same Past and Past Participle

| Present | Past | Past Participle |
|---------|------|-----------------|
| make | made | made |
| bring | brought | brought |
| sleep | slept | slept |
| catch | caught | caught |
| find | found | found |
| think | thought | thought |

### Same Present and Past Participle

| Present | Past | Past Participle |
|---------|------|-----------------|
| run | ran | run |
| come | came | come |

## Your Turn

**Use the correct form of the verb in parentheses to complete each sentence.**

1. I awoke with a start and _____ (find) everything covered with snow.

2. I had _____ (sleep) soundly in spite of the raging storm.

3. The blizzard had _____ (catch) us by surprise.

4. Our animals had all _____ (run) away.

5. Father _____ (think) they would be safe outdoors.

6. He usually _____ them indoors at night.

7. Now the animals have to be _____ (catch) before they get hurt.

8. I _____ (think) catching them will keep us busy all day.

**Underline the main verb in each sentence. Rewrite the sentence using either the past or the past participle of each verb. Remember to use a form of *have* with a past participle.**

9. Mother makes butter and soap.

_____

10. John and I find many treasures in the woods.

_____

11. Darla thinks playing outside is unladylike.

_____

12. Father brings blueberries for supper.

_____

13. The neighbors come to build the barn.

_____

14. We catch fireflies in the summer.

_____

15. My friends run through the stream in hot weather.

_____

16. The cat sleeps in the loft.

_____

 **Editing** Mina included the diary of a colonial farm girl as part of her story. Find and correct eight mistakes in the use of verbs.

| Mistakes | |
|---|---|
| Capitalization | 2 |
| Punctuation | 1 |

I had sleeped late, so I ran to do my chores. Father makes me something to eat at school. On the way there, I catched a frog. My brother John say I should take it to school. I knew mrs. Frome, my teacher, would not think that was a good idea. last year I finded a snake in the woods. I taked it to school in my lunch pail. But somehow that snake come out, and the teacher ran out of the school She made me write on my slate: I will not bring snakes to school. I thinks I should not bring any more animals to school!

# IRREGULAR VERBS, PART 2

## Become a Super Writer

Mel is writing a news report for the sports section of the school paper.

*The Blue Jays swimmed to victory! Last night they won the division championship.*

When Mel reread his first sentence, *swimmed* didn't sound right. He remembered that *swim* is an **irregular verb**. The past form of *swim* is *swam*. Mel corrected the verb.

### Definition · Usage

Every verb has four principal parts.

- The past participle of some **irregular verbs** is formed by adding *n* to the present.
- Other irregular verbs have *i* in the present, *a* in the past, and *u* in the past participle.

## PRINCIPAL PARTS OF IRREGULAR VERBS

| Present | Past | Past Participle | Present | Past | Past Participle |
|---------|------|-----------------|---------|------|-----------------|
| give | gave | given | sing | sang | sung |
| take | took | taken | drink | drank | drunk |
| blow | blew | blown | ring | rang | rung |
| know | knew | known | swim | swam | swum |
| grow | grew | grown | begin | began | begun |
| throw | threw | thrown | | | |

## Your Turn

**Underline the main verb in each sentence. Write the correct form of the verb on the line.**

1. Until last night, no one know how good our team was. _____

2. They have give their best effort in the past. _____

3. It take a lot of training to win. _____

4. The meet begin at noon. _____

5. We thought they had blow it by arriving late. _____

6. But the team swim well anyway. _____

7. After the victory, the crowds had begin

   to celebrate. _____

**Fill in the blank with the correct verb form. Solve the crossword puzzle with the answers.**

**Across**

1. Joe _____ (take) first place.

3. Our track team has _____ (grow) every year.

4. The wind has _____ (blow) the runner off course.

5. Last week, Fiona _____ (swim) her best ever!

7. Ms. Kaminski _____ (give) Brooke a pat on the back after the race.

**Down**

1. The baseball pitcher will _____ (throw) a fastball.

2. Bob _____ (drink) a lot of water before every game.

6. At yesterday's game, the choir _____ (sing) during half time.

**Editing**  Edit this paragraph of Mel's news story. Find and correct six mistakes in the use of verbs.

| Mistakes | |
|---|---|
| Capitalization | 2 |
| Spelling | 5 |

I think the Blue Jays swimmed great at Saturday's meet. Everyone giving his or her best. The coach deserves a lot of credit, too. Ms. Kaminski has taked time for everyone. She known how to win a swim meet. She has give individual advice to each and every team member. She rings a bell and throws confetti when a person does a good job. all our swimers have growed under her leedership. I say, "Hats off to Ms. kaminski. She has done a super job!"

# SUBJECT-VERB AGREEMENT

## Become a Super Writer

Liz wrote these sentences in her report about sea animals.

*The dolphin lives in the sea. Dolphins swim extremely well.*

The subject of Liz's first sentence is singular, so she used a singular verb: *lives*. Since the subject of her second sentence is plural, she used a plural verb: *swim*. Liz might have written:

*The dolphin and the whale live in the sea.*

This sentence has a compound subject, so it needs a plural verb.

---

**Definition · Usage**

The **subject** and the **verb** in a sentence must agree in number.
- If the subject of a sentence is singular, use a singular verb.
- If the subject is plural, use a plural verb.

---

## Your Turn

**Underline each subject. Then write the present-tense form of the verb in parentheses to complete the sentence.**

1. Porpoises, dolphins, and whales _____ to the order Cetacea. (belong)

2. The porpoise _____ waters near the coast to the open sea. (prefer)

3. Porpoises, which are very social animals, _____ in great herds. (gather)

4. Like other mammals, a baby porpoise _____ its mother's milk. (drink)

5. All mammals _____ air through their lungs. (breathe)

6. Blubber _____ the porpoise's body heat in cold water. (conserve)

7. A dolphin _____ squeaks, grunts, and clicks to communicate. (use)

8. Scientists _____ dolphins may be able to communicate with us. (think)

9. These marine animals _____ their way around in the ocean depths. (find)

10. A baby dolphin and its mother _____ a close bond. (form)

11. The mother and her companions _____ the baby from harm. (protect)

12. The companions _____ the baby up for its first breath of air. (push)

**Underline the correct form of the verb in parentheses. Then circle it in the word-search puzzle. Double-check your work by drawing a line from each verb to its subject.**

13. The arms of a jellyfish (shoot, shoots) poison.

14. Flying fish (live, lives) in the sea.

15. The dolphin (breathe, breathes) air.

16. A shell (cover, covers) an oyster's whole body.

17. Oysters (fasten, fastens) themselves to rocks.

18. Squids' shells (form, forms) inside their bodies.

19. A coral's arms (catch, catches) tiny animals that swim nearby.

20. Starfish (grow, grows) new arms.

21. The starfish (see, sees) only dark and light.

22. Whales (dive, dives) into deep parts of the ocean.

23. A giant squid (wrap, wraps) its legs around a whale and (squeeze, squeezes).

24. People (hunt, hunts) whales for meat and oil.

| a | k | n | e | e | r | g | l | y | d | i |
|---|---|---|---|---|---|---|---|---|---|---|
| p | e | b | l | p | b | w | r | a | p | s |
| f | o | r | m | a | n | s | o | o | n | h |
| l | n | e | e | c | r | l | g | b | w | o |
| y | e | a | h | a | o | i | j | e | d | o |
| i | t | t | u | t | d | v | f | a | s | t |
| n | s | h | n | c | i | e | e | v | e | z |
| a | a | e | t | h | v | w | c | r | e | l |
| b | f | s | q | u | e | e | z | e | s | t |

 **Editing**   Edit this paragraph from Liz's report. Find and correct six verbs that do not agree with their subjects.

| Mistakes | |
|---|---|
| Capitalization | 2 |
| Punctuation | 1 |

The blue whale measure more than 100 feet in length. This mammal weighs about 125 tons Blue whales lives mostly in the Pacific Ocean. Believe it or not, they have no teeth! Instead of teeth, their mouths have a special structure. It consist of bony plates. we call the structure a baleen. It grow down from the roof of the whale's mouth. It forms a kind of sieve. A blue whale swims with its mouth open. little fish enter the whale's mouth. The whale close its mouth. The water go out, but "dinner" stays in.

# CHANGE OF TENSE

## Become a Super Writer

Joe is writing a report about the weather. He began with these sentences.

*It rained all day yesterday. It rained the day before and the day before that. The forecast predicts more rain tomorrow. When will it stop?*

Joe used three tenses: past *(rained)*, present *(predicts)*, and future *(will stop)*. Joe used these tenses correctly. What he wrote required **a change of tense**.

**Definition · Usage**

Tense tells when the action of a verb takes place. Use the same tense for all verbs in a sentence or paragraph—unless a **change of tense** is needed to make the meaning clear.

## Your Turn

**Read these pairs of sentences. If both verbs are in the same tense, and make sense, write *correct*. If there's an unnecessary change of tense, cross out one verb. Write the correct form of the verb.**

1. Water vapor condenses high above the ground. Clouds formed. _____

2. Cloud droplets grow larger. They become heavy. _____

3. Air currents cannot hold the droplets up. They fall to the ground. _____

4. We knew the falling droplets as rain. We call frozen droplets snow. _____

5. Weather forecasters study fronts. Fronts were like boundary lines. _____

6. Cold air moves south. Warm air will move north from the tropics. _____

7. Cold air meets warm air. This meeting place makes up the front. _____

8. Rain brings needed water to the earth. It fills our lakes and streams. _____

9. A rainstorm will spoil plans for a picnic. It will also clean the air. _____

10. There was a rainbow in the sky this morning. It looks beautiful! _____

**Read the sentence pairs. If the verb tense is wrong, rewrite one of the sentences with the correct verb. Write *correct* if the verb tense does not need to be changed.**

**11.** We know February 2 as Groundhog Day. Groundhogs will sleep all winter.

_____

**12.** A groundhog appears on February 2. It sees its shadow.

_____

**13.** The groundhog will run back into its burrow. It wants more sleep.

_____

**14.** There are six weeks more of winter. That was bad news!

_____

**15.** I think this is a silly superstition. Most people agree with me.

_____

**16.** Some groundhogs slept past February 2. Cold keeps them in their burrows.

_____

**17.** The superstition started in Europe. It came to America with the Pilgrims.

_____

**18.** This February 2, I will listen to a weather report on TV. It will give me a scientific weather forecast.

_____

 **Editing**  Edit this paragraph from Joe's report. Correct four verb tenses.

| Mistakes | | |
|---|---|---|
| | Capitalization | 1 |
| | Punctuation | 1 |
| | Spelling | 5 |

In the past, peeple tried to control whether. Some people still tried to control it today. Scientists control rain through "cloud seeding." They spray chemicals into clouds. Sometimes, they dropped chemicals into clouds from airplains. Sometimes, they release the chemicals from the ground. Wind carried the chemicals up into the clouds, the chemicals cause rain droplets in the clouds to fall. Not everyone will think cloud seeding is a good idea. Most states in the United States regulate cloud seeding. Recently, severel states have even made it agenst the law.

# PROBLEM VERBS AND WORDS

## Become a Super Writer

Astrid is writing a report about the use of computers. She wrote:

*A computer may help us in many ways. For one, it don't get tired.*

In revising her sentences, Astrid changed *may* to *can* and *don't* to *doesn't*.

*A computer can help us in many ways. For one, it doesn't get tired.*

### Definition · Usage

Some verbs are confusing because they are close in meaning or because some of their principal parts look alike.
**Don't** and **Doesn't** must agree with their subject.
**Don't** is used with *I, we,* and *they* or nouns that these pronouns could replace.
**Doesn't** is used with *he, she* or *it* or nouns that these pronouns could replace.

| VERB | MEANING | VERB | MEANING |
|------|---------|------|---------|
| can | to be able | let | to allow |
| may | to have permission | leave | to depart |
| set | to put in place | lie | to recline |
| sit | to occupy a seat | lay | to place or put down |

## Your Turn

**Underline the word you would use to correctly complete each sentence.**

1. With word processing, you (can, may) write stories on a computer.

2. The computer (lets, leaves) you make many changes.

3. Most writers (let, leave) spell-checking until the end.

4. The spell-checking tool is good, but it (doesn't, don't) know if a word is misused.

5. A student (sits, sets) down story ideas in a first draft.

6. He or she (can, may) then delete, insert, or move words around.

7. Most people (set, sit) in a comfortable chair in front of the computer.

8. (Lie, Lay) your books close to you for easy reference.

**If the word in bold type is correct, write *correct* on the line. If the word is incorrect, cross it out. Write the correct word on the line.**

9. As a kid, Nolan Bushnell **set** for hours with a computer game. _____

10. Nolan had **learned** to play *Spacewar*, and he thought it was great. _____

11. "Why **don't** someone make more of these games?" Nolan wondered. _____

12. Nolan said, "I'm smart. I **may** do it myself!" _____

13. He **sat** down plans for a computer game company. _____

14. **Doesn't** you know his company—Atari? _____

15. Today people **may** play computer games in arcades or at home. _____

16. Some games **leave** you travel in space or play hockey with the pros. _____

17. Realistic computer images **sit** players in the middle of the action. _____

18. Even with all that computers can do, they **can't** think. _____

19. Without human input, the computer just **lays** there. _____

20. It **don't** do a thing until a person tells it to. _____

**Editing** Read the following paragraph from Astrid's report. Correct five errors in the use of problem verbs and words.

| Mistakes | | |
|---|---|---|
| | Capitalization | 1 |
| | Punctuation | 1 |
| | Spelling | 4 |

In some homes, kids set down in front of the computer for ours. In others, children may use the computer only at certain times for a limited period. otherwise some kids would lay awake in bed with their laptops all nite long. Peopel can easily become computer junkies. The computer don't say, "That's all for today, folks." The computer just leaves you play as long as you want? The Internet don't ever cloze!

# VERBS AND TENSES

Circle the action verb in each newspaper headline. Write *past*, *present*, or *future* to tell the tense of the verb.

1. Local Fifth Graders Win Writing Contest _____

2. Police Stopped Suspects at the Bridge _____

3. Firefighters Rescue Kitten in Tree _____

4. Mayor Throws Hat in Ring for Reelection _____

5. Tennis Player Will Take Opponent to Court _____

6. County Will Vote on New Courthouse _____

7. No One Appears at Memory-Improvement Class _____

8. Citizens March for Automobile Safety _____

9. PTA Will Hold Craft Show _____

10. Cyclist Sought Help Before Accident _____

**These sentences were taken from signs. Circle each helping verb and underline the main verb.**

11. Police will tow all parked cars.

12. Casey's Pet Shop has moved next door.

13. Patrons can drop old clothing in this bin.

14. This store is closing on Thursday.

15. All passengers shall show photo I.D.

16. Owners will curb their dogs—or else.

17. All students will report at 8 A.M.

18. Bonker's has gone out of business.

**Write a linking verb to complete each ad. Choose from *be*, *appear*, *look*, *taste*, *feel*, and *seem*.**

19. You _____ a guest, not a customer, at Friendly Fred's.

20. You will _____ like a king at Royalty Restaurant.

21. Does your life sometimes _____ hectic?

22. Yogurt never _____ so good.

23. You will _____ younger after a facial by Felicia.

**Use the verbs in parentheses to complete these story titles. Be sure to write the correct principal part of the verb.**

24. (Dial) You Have _____ for the Last Dime

25. (Paint) Pete Is _____ the Fence Posts

26. (Walk) Who Has _____ Down That Path?

27. (Go) Willie _____ Wild Last Wednesday

28. (Take) I Have _____ That Bus Before

29. (Become) How I _____ a Soccer Star

30. (Sing) You Have _____ Too Loud Too Often

31. (Catch) We _____ a Falling Star

**Rewrite the answers to these riddles so that subjects and verbs agree.**

32. How can you tell when elephants have headaches?
    They wears ice packs on their heads.

    _____

33. What's the difference between a doctor and an elephant?
    One carry a little black bag; the other carry a trunk.

    _____

34. Two polar bears are both red and white. What's the matter?
    The bear and its twin has the measles.

    _____

**Each pair of far-out facts has a problem with a change in verb tense. Edit the sentences so that the verbs are correct.**

35. Honey never spoils. Honey from tombs of ancient Egypt still tasted good today.

36. Lorenzo Amato set a record in 1978. His pizza will weigh a total of 18,664 pounds.

**Edit these sayings. Write the correct verb or verb form on the line.**

37. <u>Leave</u> sleeping dogs lie. _____

38. A rolling stone <u>gather</u> no moss. _____

39. A stitch in time <u>save</u> nine. _____

40. You can't <u>learn</u> an old dog new tricks. _____

NAME _____

# VERBS AND TENSES

**For each sentence, fill in the circle below the action verb.**

1. The <u>glacier</u> <u>slowly</u> <u>flowed</u> <u>down</u> the mountainside.
   ○         ○         ○         ○

2. It <u>carried</u> large <u>amounts</u> of <u>rock</u> and <u>soil</u>.
   ○                    ○              ○           ○

**For each sentence, fill in the circle below the helping verb.**

3. We <u>are</u> <u>touring</u> the Alaskan coast <u>on</u> a cruise <u>ship</u>.
   ○      ○                              ○              ○

4. Our ship <u>has</u> <u>sailed</u> for <u>miles</u> up and <u>down</u> the coast.
   ○      ○              ○                 ○

**For each sentence, fill in the circle below the main verb.**

5. You <u>can</u> <u>see</u> <u>icebergs</u> <u>from</u> the boat's observation deck.
   ○    ○      ○          ○

6. I <u>will</u> <u>write</u> a <u>description</u> in my diary <u>tonight</u>.
   ○    ○          ○                        ○

**For each sentence, fill in the circle below the linking verb.**

7. That <u>iceberg</u> <u>looks</u> <u>very</u> <u>dangerous</u>!
   ○          ○        ○        ○

8. The <u>sea</u> air <u>tastes</u> a <u>little</u> bit <u>salty</u>.
   ○          ○            ○          ○

**For each sentence, fill in the circle by the answer that tells the verb tense.**

9. We will sail on to Kodiak, Alaska, tomorrow.
   ○ past        ○ present        ○ future

10. Brown bears live on the island of Kodiak.
    ○ past        ○ present        ○ future

11. Dad told me about the rush for gold in the Klondike.
    ○ past        ○ present        ○ future

**Fill in the circle by the verb or verb phrase that correctly completes each sentence.**

12. Last night, Mom and I _____ up onto the deck of the ship.

    ○ were going    ○ go    ○ will go    ○ gone

13. Something _____ in the water below.

    ○ have splashed    ○ splashed    ○ splashing    ○ will splash

14. I _____ I would spot a whale on this trip, but I did!

    ○ thought    ○ hadn't thought    ○ isn't thinking    ○ hadn't thinked

**Fill in the circle by the sentence in which the subject and the verb agree.**

15. ○ Forests cover about one third of Alaska.

    ○ Forests covers about one third of Alaska.

16. ○ Herds of musk oxen live on Nunivak Island.

    ○ Herds of musk oxen lives on Nunivak Island.

17. ○ Salmon and halibut swims in the coastal waters.

    ○ Salmon and halibut swim in the coastal waters.

**Fill in the circle by the sentence in which the tense does not change.**

18. ○ The U. S. bought Alaska from Russia, and it became a state in 1959.

    ○ The U. S. buys Alaska from Russia, and it became a state in 1959.

19. ○ My cousins will visit Alaska next summer, and I shall travel with them.

    ○ My cousins will visit Alaska next summer, and I travel with them.

**Fill in the circle by the correct verb to complete each sentence.**

20. I _____ the book about Alaska on the table.

    ○ sat    ○ set    ○ sit    ○ have sat

21. You _____ borrow the book if you'd like.

    ○ can    ○ may    ○ don't    ○ leave

22. Last night, I _____ awake thinking about the trip.

    ○ lie    ○ lay    ○ laid    ○ lain

# COMMON, PROPER, AND PREDICATE ADJECTIVES

## Become a Super Writer

Hal was writing a letter to a friend about the Statue of Liberty.

*The history of the Statue of Liberty is* <u>interesting</u>. *The idea for it came from a* <u>French</u> *sculptor. The statue is a symbol of freedom to* <u>many</u> *people.*

The underlined words that Hal used are adjectives.

### Definitions·Usage

A **common adjective** describes a noun or pronoun. (*many* people)

A **proper adjective** is formed from a proper noun. (*French* sculptor)

A **predicate adjective** is an adjective that follows a linking verb. It describes the subject. (The history is *interesting*.)

## Your Turn

**Each underlined word is an adjective. Write *common* or *proper* to tell what kind of adjective each is. If it is also a predicate adjective, write *PA*.**

1. The <u>hundredth</u> anniversary of the Declaration of Independence was in 1876. _____

2. France wanted to give the United States a <u>special</u> gift. _____

3. War broke out in Europe, so France was too <u>busy</u> to think about the gift. _____

4. Frédéric Bartholdi, a <u>French</u> sculptor, came to New York in 1874. _____

5. When he saw New York Harbor, he got a <u>wonderful</u> inspiration. _____

6. He would design a goddess of Liberty, a <u>magnificent</u> statue. _____

7. It would be put in the harbor to welcome <u>European</u> immigrants. _____

8. The statue was <u>tall</u> (151 feet) and <u>heavy</u> (225 tons). _____

9. The sculptors assembled the statue on a pedestal in <u>Upper</u> New York Harbor. _____

10. The statue served as a symbol of friendship between France and the <u>American</u> people. _____

**Underline the adjectives in the sentences below. Then on the line write whether the adjective is common, proper, or predicate. Some sentences may have two answers.**

11. The Statue of Liberty is the largest statue in the world. _____

12. Over the years, harsh weather damaged the statue. _____

13. The tourist attraction became unsafe for visitors. _____

14. The American government spent millions of dollars on repairs.

    _____

15. In 1986, America celebrated the hundredth anniversary of the

    statue. _____

**Use adjectives from the word bank to complete these sentences.**

| talented | spectacular | copper |
|---|---|---|
| New York | gold-covered | festive |

16. The display of fireworks was _____ .

17. Forty thousand ships floated around the _____ statue.

18. Two hundred airplanes circled above the _____ torch.

19. Twenty thousand _____ performers entertained the guests.

20. The _____ celebration lasted for four days.

**Editing** Read this paragraph from Hal's letter. Fix six adjectives that are misspelled. Add some adjectives of your own.

| Mistakes | |
|---|---|
| Punctuation | 2 |

Frédéric Bartholdi designed the Statue of Liberty. He based his design on a girl he once saw. When he was a yung student, Bartholdi lived in a Fernch city The city was surrounded by a high wall. The wall was supposed to protect the city and keep out enimy soldiers. During one war, Bartholdi saw a girl jump over the wall It was night, and she carried a flameing torch. As she jumped, the girl screamed, "Forward!" Bartholdi never forgot the girl with the torch. Years later, she gave him the idea for the basik design of the faimous statue.

# DEMONSTRATIVE ADJECTIVES, ARTICLES

## Become a Super Writer

While she was in San Francisco, Connie sent her cousin a postcard. It showed Lombard Street. Here is what Connie wrote.

San Francisco is <u>a</u> great city! <u>The</u> streets here are so steep. <u>The</u> one you see here is crooked, too. (This) street is known as <u>the</u> crookedest street in <u>the</u> world.

In these sentences, Connie used articles and a demonstrative adjective. All the articles are underlined. The demonstrative adjective is circled.

**Definitions**

An **article** is an adjective.
A **demonstrative adjective** describes a noun.

### ARTICLES
a    an    the

### DEMONSTRATIVE ADJECTIVES
this        these
that        those

## Your Turn

**Underline the articles and circle the demonstrative adjectives.**

1. San Francisco was first settled by the Costanoan Indians.

2. In 1776 a Spanish expedition set up a fort in the area.

3. This expedition was led by a man named Juan Bautista de Anza.

4. Before long, Spanish priests opened a mission near the fort.

5. The mission was named in honor of a Catholic saint, Francis of Assisi.

6. Near this mission was a stream that Anza called Arroyo de los Dolores.

7. Because of this stream, the mission became known as Mission Dolores.

8. The settlement around the mission was called the Pueblo de San Francisco.

9. You can still visit the Mission District in San Francisco today.

10. This area of the city is an important tourist attraction.

11. Other popular tourist sites include the Golden Gate Bridge and Fisherman's Wharf.

Bonus:  If you can find a Spanish article, place two underlines below it.

**Read each sentence. Use proofreaders' marks to correct mistakes in the use of demonstrative adjectives and articles.**

| | | |
|---|---|---|
| ✄ | delete |
| ∧ | insert |

12. This here city has lots of interesting sights to see.

13. The Golden Gate is an one-mile-wide channel that connects a Pacific Ocean with San Francisco Bay.

14. A Golden Gate Bridge, a long suspension bridge, crosses that there channel.

15. There are steep hills in the city, and cable cars clang loudly as they climb those there hills.

16. The Lombard Street on Russian Hill is famous for its sharp S-curves, and that there street is a most crooked street in the world.

**Write five sentences to describe a place in your town or city that might interest a tourist. Underline the articles and circle any demonstrative adjectives that you use.**

17. _____

18. _____

19. _____

20. _____

21. _____

 **Editing** Connie also sent her cousin a postcard from Fisherman's Wharf. Correct seven mistakes in the use of articles and demonstrative adjectives.

| Mistakes | |
|---|---|
| Capitalization | 3 |
| Punctuation | 2 |

This there is Fisherman's Wharf, where we are having a seafood lunch. The photo on the front of this here card shows the restaurant. It's supposed to be a excellent one—except that I don't like fish. I can see the sailboats out on the bay There are also some fishing boats tied up at the wharf. Workers are unloading the "catch of the day." I spotted my "catch of the day" across an street at ghirardelli Square. It was once a chocolate factory now it's a unusual shopping center famous for its Chocolate ice cream. I decided to have dessert at that there place, not this here one!

# COMPARING WITH ADJECTIVES, PART 1

## Become a Super Writer

Justin is collecting facts for a trivia collage. Here are three of his facts.

In America, the tennis shoe is <u>more popular</u> than the cowboy boot.

The <u>shortest</u> distance from the East Coast to the West Coast is from Jacksonville, Florida, to San Diego, California—2,092 miles.

The <u>most common</u> surname in the world is *Chang*.

In writing these facts, Justin used adjectives to compare two or more things.

### Definitions · Usage

A **comparative adjective** compares two nouns or pronouns. It shows how two people, places, things, or ideas are alike or different. To make comparative forms of adjectives,
• Add the ending *er* to most shorter adjectives
• Use the word *more* before longer adjectives

A **superlative adjective** compares three or more nouns or pronouns. To make superlative forms of adjectives,
• Add the ending *est* to most shorter adjectives
• Use the word *most* before longer adjectives

## Your Turn

**Circle the adjectives used to compare. Write** *comparative* **or** *superlative* **on the line.**

1. The world's biggest clams weigh almost 500 pounds. _____

2. A newborn panda is smaller than a mouse. _____

3. The strongest muscle in your body is your tongue. _____

4. The brain of a dolphin is bigger than a human brain. _____

5. *Jack* is the most common name in nursery rhymes. _____

6. The oldest vegetable in the world is the pea. _____

7. Is Superman really faster than a speeding bullet? _____

8. Of all vegetables, the turnip is the most disliked. _____

9. The most widespread disease in the world is tooth decay. _____

**Underline the comparative or superlative adjective in each sentence. Then circle *C* if the adjective is comparative or *S* if the adjective is superlative. Use the letters next to your answers to solve the riddle below.**

10. Of all the planets, Pluto is the most distant.　　**C** (N)　or　**S** (M)

11. Pluto is also the coldest planet, with temperatures of -300˚F.　　**C** (E)　or　**S** (I)

12. Venus is closer to Earth than it is to Mars.　　**C** (L)　or　**S** (R)

13. Jupiter has fewer rings than Saturn.　　**C** (K)　or　**S** (A)

14. Earth has the largest amount of oxygen in its atmosphere.　　**C** (T)　or　**S** (Y)

15. The planets are much smaller than the sun.　　**C** (W)　or　**S** (E)

16. The moon is the brightest object in the sky at night.　　**C** (P)　or　**S** (A)

17. The oldest rock found on the moon is more than
four billion years old!　　**C** (H)　or　**S** (Y)

18. One type contains chocolate and another type contains the
sun, the earth, and hundreds of billions of stars.

$$\overline{\quad}\ \overline{\quad}\ \overline{\quad}\ \overline{\quad}\ \overline{\quad}\ \ \overline{\quad}\ \overline{\quad}\ \overline{\quad}$$
10　11　12　13　14　　15　16　17

 **Editing**　Read Justin's list of trivia questions. In each
question, correct Justin's misuse of adjectives.

| Mistakes | |
|---|---|
| Capitalization | 5 |
| Punctuation | 3 |

19. Why is *Julius Caesar's* autograph the valuablest of all autographs?

20. Which is popularer with americans, radio or television?

21. Is "Park" the commonest street name in the United states.

22. Was harry Houdini the world's great escape artist?

23. Who was the greatest conqueror, Genghis Khan or Alfred the Great?

24. Was George Armstrong Custer the most young person to become a general
in the U.S. Army.

25. Did the more destructive earthquake in the united states happen in 1906?

26. Which raced more fast in 1830, a horse or the steam locomotive *Tom Thumb*.

27. Which is the most popular pet of Americans, cats or dogs?

# COMPARING WITH ADJECTIVES, PART 2

## Become a Super Writer

Jocelyn is writing about her favorite sport, gymnastics. She wrote:

Who is the <u>best</u> female gymnast in the world? Shannon Miller won a gold medal in the 1996 Olympics for her performance on the balance beam during the event finals. She is certainly a <u>good</u> gymnast! However, Lilia Podkopayeva won the women's all-around title. Is Lilia a <u>better</u> gymnast than Shannon?

In her sentences, Jocelyn correctly used adjectives that compare—*good, better,* and *best.*

### Definitions

A **comparative adjective** compares two nouns or pronouns. A **superlative adjective** compares three or more nouns or pronouns. Some adjectives have special forms for the comparative and superlative.

| ADJECTIVE | COMPARATIVE | SUPERLATIVE |
|-----------|-------------|-------------|
| good | better | best |
| bad | worse | worst |

## Your Turn

**Use a form of *good* or *bad* to complete each sentence.**

1. To be a gymnast, you need to have _____ balance and flexibility.

2. Most gymnasts work hard to become _____ athletes.

3. The _____ gymnasts devote many hours to the balance beam and the uneven bars.

4. Which do you think is the _____ event, the balance beam or the uneven bars?

5. The _____ thing a gymnast can do is to try a handspring or a cartwheel without stretching first.

6. Forgetting to stretch your muscles can result in a _____ sprain.

7. A broken bone is an even _____ injury.

**Use the words in the word banks to complete each set of sentences.**

> good     better     best

8. Janice gave her _____ performance ever at the state championships.

9. Janice had a _____ practice today, and her coach was very pleased.

10. Janice wants to become an even _____ gymnast than she is now.

> bad     worse     worst

11. Marco took a _____ fall during his dismount from the rings.

12. He had an even _____ fall last week while he was on the high bars.

13. Marco's _____ fall was during the state competition.

**Use the words in the word banks to write sentences about a sport you like.**

14. _____

15. _____

16. _____

17. _____

18. _____

19. _____

 **Editing**    Read Jocelyn's paragraph. Correct four errors in adjective forms.

| Mistakes | |
|---|---|
| Punctuation | 3 |
| Spelling | 3 |

Someday, I hope to be as best as Shannon Miller, Shannon is my role model. I practise almost every day and I always try to do my best. My most good event so far is the floor exercises. I have taken dancing lessons and I am a good dancer I think dancing has helped me impruve my routine. My worse event is the balance beam. It is hard to keep your balance while doing triks on such a narrow beam. To be as good as Shannon, I need to work hard to be a gooder all-around gymnast than I am now.

# ADJECTIVES

**Underline eight common adjectives and three demonstrative adjectives. Circle six articles.**

On May 10, 1908, a woman named Anna Jarvis honored the memory of her mother by wearing a carnation on her blouse. She wanted to devote this special day to mothers. Six years later, her dream came true. President Woodrow Wilson declared the second Sunday in May as the official day for honoring mothers. Today, many families celebrate this holiday by sending greeting cards or pretty flowers. Others prepare a nice breakfast for Mom. These expressions of love show mothers just how wonderful they truly are!

**Write a proper adjective to complete each sentence. Use the clues in parentheses to form the adjective.**

1. The _____ Constitution protects the rights of its citizens. (your country)

2. The meal began with _____ onion soup. (France)

3. The _____ numeral for ten is X. (Rome)

4. Do you enjoy reading _____ haiku? (Japan)

5. The _____ governor spoke to our class today. (Hawaii)

**Complete each sentence with the appropriate articles.**

6. _____ ornithologist is _____ person who studies birds.

7. _____ artist Rembrandt painted _____ picture known as "Night Watch."

8. _____ apple is _____ healthier snack than _____ ice-cream cone.

9. _____ Smiths' new puppy hid under one of _____ twins' beds.

**Underline the predicate adjective in each sentence.**

10. The roar of the huge lion was ferocious.

11. Roller coasters with loops are exciting.

12. The chocolate milkshake is thick.

13. The pretty colors of the rainbow were vivid.

**Write the correct demonstrative adjective to complete each sentence. Choose from *this, that, these,* and *those*.**

14. Place the sofa next to us here on _____ side of the stage.

15. Have the actor enter from _____ side, which is opposite us.

16. What shall we do with _____ flowers I'm holding?

17. Put them in _____ vase on the far side of the stage.

18. Now, please take _____ boxes in the corner to the prop room.

**To complete each sentence, write the correct form of the adjective in parentheses.**

19. Amanda is the _____ runner in the class. (fast)

20. Lyle thinks he's the _____ guy in town. (cool)

21. Jeff is _____ than Mike by about two inches. (tall)

22. Corrine is the _____ girl I know. (artistic)

23. Jo is a _____ musician than Andrea. (accomplished)

24. The _____ boy I know is Bernie. (popular)

**Write *good, better,* or *best* to complete each sentence.**

25. Kim polled her classmates to find out what they thought the _____ show was.

26. Jim said he didn't think any of the shows he watched were very _____ .

27. Olga said she would rather read a _____ book than watch TV.

28. Lou said nature shows are _____ than sitcoms.

**Write *bad, worse,* or *worst* to complete each sentence.**

29. Mike also took a poll, but he asked which shows were the _____ .

30. He got lots of answers, but his classmates couldn't agree on the absolutely _____ show.

31. Pauline said that *Star Walk* was bad but *Moonsters* was _____ .

32. Stephanie said she would rather eat spinach than watch a _____ cooking show.

NAME _____

# ADJECTIVES

**Read each sentence. Fill in the circle under the word that is an adjective.**

1. The <u>old</u> <u>clock</u> <u>stopped</u> running at <u>midnight</u>.
   ○    ○    ○        ○

2. <u>Loud</u> <u>music</u> <u>poured</u> from the <u>basement</u>.
   ○    ○    ○      ○

3. In <u>spring</u> and <u>fall</u>, <u>nature</u> is <u>glorious</u>.
   ○    ○  ○    ○

4. There <u>is</u> a <u>problem</u> with the <u>portable</u> <u>television</u>.
   ○    ○      ○    ○

5. <u>Baseball</u> is still <u>considered</u> the <u>American</u> <u>pastime</u>.
   ○      ○      ○    ○

**Read each sentence. Fill in the circle by the sentence that contains a proper adjective.**

6. ○ The newspaper prints interesting stories and articles about life in America.

   ○ One story dealt with American inventions.

7. ○ I read a book about great Roman generals.

   ○ I like to read about the conquests of the Romans.

**Read these sentences. Fill in the circle by the sentence that contains a predicate adjective.**

8. ○ The snowfall was heavy.

   ○ The wind whistled through the trees.

9. ○ My average went up since last year.

   ○ Now I feel enthusiastic about school.

**Read each sentence. Fill in the circle by the sentence that uses articles correctly.**

10. ○ Michael took a big bite of a apple.

   ○ He saw a worm and dropped the apple.

11. ○ Leeza built a huge sandcastle surrounded by the moat.

   ○ Unfortunately, a huge wave crashed over the sandcastle.

**Choose the sentence in which demonstrative adjectives are used correctly.**

12. ○ If you look through these telescope, you can see the planet Mars.

    ○ If you look through this telescope, you can see the planet Mars.

13. ○ That planet has two moons, while this here planet has only one.

    ○ That planet has two moons, while this planet has only one.

14. ○ Those books on the table need to be returned to the library.

    ○ Those there books on the table need to be returned to the library.

**Fill in the circle by the form of the adjective that correctly completes each sentence.**

15. A book can be _____ than a movie.

    ○ scary          ○ scarier          ○ more scarier          ○ most scary

16. For many people, radio is _____ than television.

    ○ popular     ○ popularer     ○ more popular     ○ most popular

17. Exercise helps build _____ bones and muscles.

    ○ strong          ○ stronger          ○ strongest          ○ more stronger

18. The plane ride was the _____ part of the trip.

    ○ exciting     ○ excitingest     ○ more exciting     ○ most exciting

19. Of all the sections of the exam, the word problem was the _____.

    ○ tough          ○ tougher          ○ toughest          ○ most toughest

**Fill in the circle by the correct form of the adjective to complete each sentence.**

20. Who has the _____ jump shot on the team?

    ○ good     ○ better     ○ best     ○ gooder

21. Is the weather in England _____ than the weather here?

    ○ good     ○ better     ○ best     ○ gooder

22. Mark's cold is the _____ one I have ever seen.

    ○ bad     ○ worse     ○ worst     ○ badder

# ADVERBS: WHERE, WHEN, HOW

## Become a Super Writer

Paul wrote a report on thunderstorms. Here is how it began.

Thunder <u>booms</u> in the sky. The sound <u>travels</u>. People <u>believed</u> it was the sound of angry gods.

Paul added adverbs to tell more about the underlined verbs. His first adverb tells *where*, his second tells *how*, and his third tells *when*.

Thunder <u>booms high</u> in the sky. The sound <u>travels quickly</u>. People <u>once believed</u> it was the sound of angry gods.

### Definition · Usage

An **adverb** describes an action verb, an adjective, or another adverb. Most adverbs tell *where, how,* or *when* an action happens. Adverbs often end in *ly*.

## Your Turn

**Underline the adverb in each sentence. Then decide if it tells** *where, how,* **or** *when.* **Circle the letter at the right.**

|  | WHERE | HOW | WHEN |
|---|---|---|---|
| 1. Scientists today study thunder. | a | e | i |
| 2. They know its causes well. | s | t | r |
| 3. Thunder can occur anywhere. | c | h | n |
| 4. Lightning rapidly heats the sky. | b | l | d |
| 5. The air expands violently. | o | a | u |
| 6. Air molecules expand everywhere. | p | w | f |
| 7. Molecules immediately collide with cool air. | y | m | s |
| 8. An air wave then spreads. | u | e | a |
| 9. The wave thunders loudly. | t | l | f |
| 10. We hear the thunder occasionally. | s | e | o |
| 11. The sound booms above. | t | h | y |

**Write the circled letters in these spaces to learn why thunder is a great audience.**

12. ___ ___    ___ ___ ___ ___ ___    ___    ___ ___ ___
    1   2      3   4   5   6   7      8      9  10  11

**Read each sentence and the words below it. For each sentence, choose three adverbs that could be used to complete the sentence. Write all three adverbs on the line.**

13. Storm clouds form _____ in the late afternoon.
_____

| overhead | simple | sun |
| suddenly | quietly | |

14. The thunder rumbles _____ in the sky.
_____

| ocean | loudly | high |
| danger | often | |

15. The sound travels _____ for several miles.
_____

| instantly | streaks | above |
| rapidly | lightning | |

16. Lightning _____ travels faster than thunder.
_____

| always | bolts | protect |
| certainly | scarily | |

17. The sound _____ fades in the distance.
_____

| slowly | should | quick |
| eventually | surely | |

18. Thunder may occur _____ during a storm.
_____

| minute | start | often |
| noisily | suddenly | |

**Editing**    Read Paul's description of a thunderstorm. Add at least five adverbs to tell more about the verbs. Then reread the description to be sure it makes sense.

| Mistakes | |
|---|---|
| Capitalization | 2 |
| Spelling | 5 |

The sky darkuns. Gray clouds gather in bunches. A bolt of lightning streaks across the sky. Pedestrians in the Street run for cover. They duck into ofice buildings, restaurants, and other available shelters. no one stands under a tree. Lightning can strike a tree and injure a person standing under the branshes. Umbrellas open. Claps of thunder explode in the sky. Everyone scurrys in one direction or another. The thunder echoes for several minutes. The storm passes, and the sun appeers.

# COMPARING WITH ADVERBS

## Become a Super Writer

Sheila wrote a report that compared different animals. Here is part of it.

An owl flies <u>fast</u>, but an eagle flies <u>fastest</u>. A hawk flies <u>faster</u> of all.

Later, Sheila corrected the adverbs she used to make comparisons.

An owl flies <u>fast</u>, but an eagle flies <u>faster</u>. A hawk flies <u>fastest</u> of all.

### Definitions·Usage

A **comparative adverb** compares two actions. Add the ending *er* to one-syllable adverbs. Add the word *more* before longer adverbs and those that end with *ly*. (*An owl flies <u>swiftly</u>, but an eagle flies <u>more</u> <u>swiftly</u>*).

A **superlative adverb** compares more than two actions. Add the ending *est* to one-syllable adverbs. Add *most* before longer adverbs and those that end with *ly*. (*A hawk flies most swiftly of all.*)

## Your Turn

**Underline each adverb used to make a comparison. Circle the letter under *C* if it is comparative or *S* if it is superlative.**

|  |  | **C** | **S** |
|---|---|---|---|
| 1. | A turtle moves more slowly than a snake. | t | a |
| 2. | A snail moves most slowly of all three animals. | d | h |
| 3. | A sea turtle swims more quickly than a goldfish. | e | r |
| 4. | A sailfish swims most quickly of all. | l | c |
| 5. | My cat runs more gracefully than my dog. | h | u |
| 6. | My rabbit hops higher than my dog does. | e | m |
| 7. | But my dog runs farthest of all without stopping. | i | e |
| 8. | My dog also leaps most often of all my pets. | b | t |
| 9. | I can run faster than my dog at times. | a | o |
| 10. | But the dog eats fastest of everyone in the family! | s | h |

**Write the circled letters in the spaces below to find the fastest land animal.**

11. __ __ __  __ __ __ __ __ __ __
   1  2  3  4  5  6  7  8  9  10

**Write the correct form of the adverb in parentheses to complete each sentence below.**

12. The gazelle, which is a slender antelope, runs (gracefully) of all animals.
    _____

13. Poets have written (often) about the gazelle than about any other animal I know.
    _____

14. A gazelle can run about ten miles an hour (fast) than a greyhound.
    _____

15. The cheetah, however, runs (fast) of all land animals. _____

16. Almost any animal drinks water (frequently) than the gazelle does.
    _____

17. The gazelle goes (long) without water than the average animal does.
    _____

18. A gazelle by itself moves a little (fast) than a race horse with a jockey.
    _____

19. Of all the animals I can think of, I admire the gazelle (greatly).
    _____

 **Editing** Read more of Sheila's report on animals. Correct five adverbs that are used incorrectly. Reread the paragraph to be sure it makes sense.

| Mistakes | |
|---|---|
| Punctuation | 2 |
| Spelling | 5 |

How fast are animels in the air, on land, and in the water? In the air, a blue jay flies slowest than a housefly, but it flies faster than a bat  A robin moves most swiftly than a blue jay by about ten miles an our. On land, an ostrich does not run more swiftly than a gray fox or a greyhound, but a rabit moves more swiftly of all four animals. In the watir, a barracuda swims swiftlier than a dolfin, but the tuna moves most swiftliest of all three fish?

# PROBLEM WORDS good, well; very, real

## Become a Super Writer

Steve wrote a report about beavers and how they build. He wrote:

Beavers are good builders. They use trees, sticks, and mud to build dams. Their dams are built well, but still the beavers keep a very careful lookout. A leak could be a real problem in a dam that is also a home.

The underlined words cause problems for many writers. It's easy to confuse *good* and *well*. It's also easy to confuse *very* and *real*. Steve used all four of these words in his paragraph, and he used the words correctly.

**Definition**

The **problem words** *good* and *well* and *real* and *very* are often misused.

### PROBLEM WORDS

| | |
|---|---|
| Use *good* to describe a noun. | Beavers are good builders. |
| Use *well* to describe a verb. | Beavers build their dams well. |
| Use *real* to describe a noun. | A leak is a real problem. |
| Use *very* to describe an adjective or adverb. | Keep a very careful lookout. |

## Your Turn

**Decide if each boldfaced word is used correctly. If it is, write *correct* on the line. If it is not, cross the word out and write the correct word on the line.**

1. Most beavers keep themselves **real** busy. _____

2. Beavers work **very** hard to make their homes. _____

3. A beaver's four front teeth are **real** long and strong. _____

4. They are **very well** suited for cutting down trees. _____

5. A beaver can cut down a small tree **real** fast. _____

6. A bigger tree is no **real** problem; it just takes a little longer. _____

7. Aspens and willows are **good** trees for cutting. _____

8. Their wood is soft, and the beaver can cut them **real** easily. _____

**Underline the word in parentheses that correctly completes each sentence. Then use *good, well, very,* and *real* in two sentences of your own.**

9. Another (good/well) builder in the animal kingdom is the ant.

10. Ants, which are (very/real) social insects, live in colonies.

11. They create (good/well) homes for themselves by working together.

12. Their colonies have (very/real) many rooms and connecting tunnels.

13. The nurseries in a colony are (good/well) places for young ants.

14. There are special rooms for when the weather is (very/real) cold.

15. Honeybees are also (very/real) clever home-builders.

16. Called a hive, a honeybee's home is a (very/real) marvel.

17. Each bee has a task to do, and the bees do their jobs (good/well).

18. Worker bees work (very/real) hard to build the honeycomb.

19. Other bees, called foragers, are (very/real) good at finding food.

20. Honey right from a honeycomb tastes so (good/well)!

21. _____

22. _____

**Editing** Read more of Steve's report about beavers. Correct three problem words that are used incorrectly.

| Mistakes | | |
|---|---|---|
| | Capitalization | 1 |
| | Punctuation | 2 |
| | Spelling | 5 |

From early spring untill late in the fall, beavers are real busy creatures. Spring floods may have caused a leak in their dam. that's a real problem. The beavers work real hard to make repairs. The lodje may need to be enlarged to make room for baby beavers. It's also a good ideah for the colony to store up some food for winter. Can you guess what beavers eat. They eat trees! Beavers feed good on the leeves, twigs, bark, and roots of trees. They also eat water plants. They think water lilys taste especially good.

# NEGATIVES AND DOUBLE NEGATIVES

## Become a Super Writer

Gretchen wrote a description of her visit to the White House.

I had <u>not</u> <u>never</u> seen the White House before.

The words *not* and *never* are negatives. Both words mean "no." Gretchen saw that she had used two negatives to express her idea, when only one was necessary. She corrected her double negative.

I had <u>never</u> seen the White House before.

**Definition**

A **negative** is a word that means "no." A **double negative** is the incorrect use of two negatives in the same sentence.

**NEGATIVES**

| | |
|---|---|
| no | no one |
| not | nobody |
| none | nothing |
| never | neither |

## Your Turn

**Underline the negative word or words in each sentence. If the sentence contains a double negative, write DN on the line.**

_____ 1. No one in my family had ever seen the White House before.

_____ 2. We did not know none of the things they taught us during our visit.

_____ 3. For example, I did not know that the White House has 132 rooms.

_____ 4. Nobody had never told me that it used to be called the President's House.

_____ 5. I did not know neither that it officially became the "White House" in 1902.

_____ 6. Before our visit, I had never read nothing about the White House.

_____ 7. None of my family had ever heard of the person who designed the original building.

_____ 8. His last name was not White; it was Hoban, believe it or not.

_____ 9. James Hoban wasn't no native-born American, but he was a noted architect.

_____ 10. Hoban came from Ireland, and his design was based on a building located in Ireland, not here.

**Underline the word that correctly completes each sentence.**

11. George Washington did not (ever, never) live in the President's House.

12. Washington is the only President who didn't (ever, never) live there.

13. I hadn't (any, no) idea that John Adams was the first one to live there.

14. When the Adamses moved in, the house wasn't yet finished (either, neither).

15. Mrs. Adams used the East Room to dry laundry, and nobody did (anything, nothing) to stop her.

16. Thomas Jefferson (didn't, didn't not) care that the house was "big enough for two emperors."

17. When Jefferson's wife died, there wasn't (anyone, no one) to act as hostess.

18. (Anybody, Nobody) minded when Dolley Madison offered to be the hostess.

19. She (did, didn't) not know that her husband James would be President next.

20. There wasn't (anything, nothing) left of the Madison furnishings when the house burned in 1814.

21. Dolley saved (anything, nothing) except a portrait of George Washington.

22. I saw that portrait in the East Room, not hanging in (some, no) museum.

 **Editing**    Read more of Gretchen's description. Correct three uses of double negatives.

| Mistakes | |
|---|---|
| Capitalization | 2 |
| Spelling | 5 |

A vist to the white House is a real thrill. Sadly, tourists don't get to see the whole manshun. Everyone who gos to washington wants to see the White House. There would be people wandering around all day long, and no one would get no work dun. Besides the East Room, we saw the Red, Blue, and Green rooms. Nobody didn't warn me about the State Dining Room. I couldn't never imagine haveing 140 people as guests for dinner at one time. Could you?

# ADVERBS

**Underline the adverb in each sentence.**

1. Animals watch carefully for enemies of all kinds.
2. They quickly defend themselves in an attack.
3. Bears kick powerfully with their clawed feet.
4. Moose use their horns well in a battle.
5. Clams close tightly in their shells.

**Write whether each underlined adverb tells where, when, or how.**

6. Rabbits hop <u>away</u> in dangerous situations. _____
7. Porcupines <u>bravely</u> jab their enemies with quills. _____
8. Electric eels give off a shock <u>immediately</u>. _____
9. Some snakes <u>quietly</u> bite their enemies. _____
10. Sharks bite <u>underwater</u> with powerful jaws. _____

**Underline each adverb that makes a comparison.**

11. Camels can go longer without water than other animals do.
12. They survive desert heat more easily than other creatures.
13. I rate camels highest on my list of favorite animals.
14. A camel walks most proudly of all animals, I believe.
15. It carries heavy loads farther than many other animals can.

**Write the correct form of the adverb in parentheses.**

16. A dromedary camel stands (tall) than a pony or even an adult horse.

    _____

17. The camel moves (steadily) of all the desert animals I can think of.

    _____

18. A camel survives (long) in the desert without food or water than a

    horse does. _____

19. But the camel also behaves (unpredictably) of all the desert animals.

    _____

**Underline the word in parentheses that completes the sentence correctly.**

20. A green plant needs to receive sufficient sunlight in order to grow (good, well).

21. Also, a plant cannot stay (real, very) healthy unless it receives enough water and fertilizer.

22. I felt so (good, well) when one of my slow-growing green plants suddenly burst into bloom.

23. Plants also need a (well, good) amount of fresh air in order to thrive.

24. Always pot your plants in (very, real) good soil that has lots of nutrients and good drainage.

**Underline the negative word in each sentence.**

25. Green plants will die with no air, sun, or water.

26. Never leave your plant in a stuffy room.

27. Do not keep it far away from the window.

28. Your plant will grow if you do nothing wrong.

29. Nobody wants to see a plant shrivel up.

**Choose the word in parentheses that completes the sentence correctly. Write your choice on the line.**

30. There is not (no one, anyone) in our family who grows plants like Mom. _____

31. She does not let (nothing, anything) get in the way of her planting and pruning. _____

32. I have not (ever, never) seen a plant fail to bloom under her care. _____

33. Mom does not merely plant something and then walk away from it, (either, neither). _____

34. Instead she tends to it daily so it has (not, none) of the problems that other plants might develop. _____

NAME _____

# ADVERBS

**Read each sentence. Fill in the circle below the underlined word that is an adverb.**

1. Members <u>of</u> the <u>cat</u> family <u>boldly</u> <u>roam</u> the jungle.
   ○          ○              ○          ○

2. The lion <u>roars</u> <u>loudly</u> <u>across</u> the <u>plain</u>.
   ○          ○          ○              ○

3. The <u>stripes</u> of the tiger <u>hide</u> <u>it</u> <u>well</u> in the tall grass.
   ○                        ○     ○    ○

4. The panther <u>sits</u> <u>high</u> <u>on</u> a <u>mountaintop</u>.
   ○       ○     ○          ○

**Fill in the circle to identify whether each underlined adverb tells when, where, or how.**

5. The leopard wears its coat <u>proudly</u>.      ○ when     ○ where     ○ how

6. The panther screeches <u>often</u> in the tree.   ○ when     ○ where     ○ how

7. The jaguar sits <u>low</u> in the grass and waits.  ○ when     ○ where     ○ how

8. The cheetah runs <u>swiftly</u> through the
   thick jungle.                                 ○ when     ○ where     ○ how

**Fill in the circle by the answer that correctly completes each sentence.**

9. No other kind of cat runs _____ than the cheetah.

   ○ fastest        ○ more faster        ○ most fastest        ○ faster

10. In fact, the cheetah runs _____ of all land animals.

    ○ fastest       ○ more faster        ○ most fastest        ○ faster

11. A cat serves _____ as a pet than a lion does.

    ○ easily        ○ more easily        ○ most easily        ○ most easily

12. My kitten sleeps _____ than my dog does.

    ○ more longer   ○ most longest       ○ longest            ○ longer

**Fill in the circle by the word that completes each sentence correctly.**

13. Three things help you stay in _____ condition.

    ○ good      ○ goodly      ○ weller      ○ very

14. Proper exercise works _____ for a healthy body.

    ○ real      ○ very      ○ good      ○ well      ○ bad

15. Also, eat foods that are _____ for you.

    ○ bad      ○ well      ○ good      ○ very      ○ gooder

16. Getting enough sleep is also _____ important.

    ○ very      ○ real      ○ verily      ○ bad      ○ well

17. Exercise, sleep, and nutrition are the _____ keys to success.

    ○ very      ○ well      ○ badly      ○ really      ○ real

**Fill in the circle by the sentence in each group that is written correctly.**

18. ○ Most fruits and vegetables are not never bad to eat.

    ○ Most fruits and vegetables are not ever bad to eat.

    ○ Most fruits and vegetables aren't not ever bad to eat.

    ○ Most fruits and vegetables aren't not never bad to eat.

    ○ Most fruits and vegetables aren't never bad to eat.

19. ○ I never heard no doctor say that a carrot was dangerous.

    ○ I ever heard no doctor say that a carrot was dangerous.

    ○ I never heard no doctor not say that a carrot was dangerous.

    ○ I never heard no doctor say that a carrot was not dangerous.

    ○ I never heard any doctor say that a carrot was dangerous.

20. ○ There is not nothing better than a well-balanced diet.

    ○ There isn't not nothing better than a well-balanced diet.

    ○ There is not anything better than a well-balanced diet.

    ○ There isn't not anything better than a well-balanced diet.

    ○ There is no nothing better than a well-balanced diet.

# SUBJECT AND OBJECT PRONOUNS

## Become a Super Writer

Ana was writing an article about Eric Li Cheung, a coin expert.

*Eric Li Cheung is the whiz kid of coin collecting. Eric has written articles about his hobby. Eric has taught courses on his hobby.*

Ana reread her last sentence. She realized that she had repeated the name *Eric* and the words *his hobby*. She replaced these words with pronouns.

*Eric has written articles about his hobby. He has taught courses on it.*

**Usage**

> A **subject pronoun** is used as the subject of a sentence. It replaces a noun. An **object pronoun** is used to replace a noun that follows an action verb or after words such as *to, for, in* and *with*.

**SUBJECT  PRONOUNS**

| I | you | he | she |
|---|-----|-----|-----|
| it | we | they | |

**OBJECT  PRONOUNS**

| me | you | him | her |
|----|-----|-----|-----|
| it | us | them | |

## Your Turn

**Circle the pronoun in the second sentence that refers back to the underlined words in the first sentence. Write each circled pronoun on the correct money chest below.**

1. <u>Eric</u> is our youngest coin expert. He has collected coins since he was four.

2. <u>Eric's interest</u> began with a gift. It started with an old half dollar.

3. Eric admired <u>the treasure</u>. The boy decided to look into the history behind it.

4. <u>The first coins</u> were made 3,000 years ago. They were lumps of gold or silver.

5. Rare coins are exciting to <u>Eric Li Cheung</u>. Old coins are also thrilling to him.

6. <u>Eric and I</u> know that brand new coins are special. We treat them with care.

7. If you want to know more, contact <u>this writer</u>. You can contact me by E-mail.

**SUBJECT**

**OBJECT**

**For each pair of sentences, choose a pronoun from the word banks that can take the place of the underlined words. Write the pronouns.**

| SUBJECT PRONOUNS | | | |
|---|---|---|---|
| I | you | he | she |
| it | we | they | |

| OBJECT PRONOUNS | | | |
|---|---|---|---|
| me | you | him | her |
| it | us | them | |

8. If you want to collect coins, get <u>a book</u>. Read _____ before buying coins.

9. <u>Many coin books</u> are price guides. _____ tell the value of coins.

10. Other books tell <u>readers like you</u> about the history of coins. Books about ancient or foreign coins are available to _____ .

11. <u>Eric</u> gets his coins from many places. _____ shops at dealers' and coin shows.

12. Some local coin clubs help <u>kids</u> get started. They may give _____ free coins.

13. Some kids get <u>coins</u> as birthday gifts. _____ can be good gifts to get from aunts and uncles.

14. <u>Your father</u> may have loose change in a pocket. _____ might let you look for an interesting coin.

15. <u>Your mother</u> might let you look for coins in a change purse. But be sure to ask _____ for permission first.

 **Editing** Read this paragraph about coin care. Replace the five underlined words and phrases with subject or object pronouns.

| Mistakes | |
|---|---|
| Punctuation | 2 |
| Spelling | 5 |

Coins can last for hundreds of years. Still, <u>a collector like you</u> should treat <u>the coins</u> with extra care. Eric thinks it is important to keep valuable coins in a safe place. <u>Eric</u> suggests storeing <u>valuable coins</u> in a safe. Always handel a coin by its edges to protect the coin's face. Never touch the coin's face with bare fingers. You can use small plastic bags to store coins. Coin dealers often use plastic blocks to encase verry valuable coins Sometimes a valuable coin is not protected in plastic. Do not handle <u>the valuable coin</u> unless you are waring gloves?

NAME _____

# Using I and me

## Become a Super Writer

Craig is writing his autobiography. He wrote:

*There is one thing you should know about Craig. Craig loves to sail!*

When Craig reread his sentences, he realized they sounded silly. He recalled that most autobiographies are written in the first person, so he revised his sentences. He used the personal pronouns *I* and *me* instead of his own name.

*There is one thing you should know about <u>me</u>. <u>I</u> love to sail!*

### Definition · Usage

The words *I* and *me* are **personal pronouns**.
- Use *I* as the subject of a sentence.
- Use *me* after action verbs or words like *to, in, from, at,* and *of.* It doesn't matter if the subject or object is simple or compound.

## Your Turn

**Read these sentences. If the personal pronouns are used correctly, write** *correct.* **If they are not, cross them out and write the correct pronouns on the lines.**

1. When I was just a little kid, I was afraid of the water. _____

2. Then one summer my sister taught I how to swim. _____

3. Once me could swim, I didn't want to get out of the water. _____

4. Last year, Dad said, "Me will teach you how to sail a boat." _____

5. I thought that sounded neat, and so did my sister. _____

6. The first day on the water, me was scared. _____

7. The wind made the boat heel, and I didn't like that. _____

8. My sister and me both thought we'd tip over. _____

9. Then Dad showed my sister and I some tricks. _____

10. She and me learned to let some wind out of the sails. _____

11. Sailing didn't seem so scary to me then. _____

12. Now you can't get her or I out of the sailboat! _____

**Write either the subject pronoun _I_ or the object pronoun _me_ to complete each sentence.**

13. My sister and _____ like to sail in the summer.

14. Sometimes, she and _____ enter races in the harbor.

15. Most of the time, she beats _____ to the first mark, a buoy or other object in the water.

16. Sailing around a mark is hard for most people but not for _____ .

17. After the first mark, _____ am usually in the lead.

18. Of course, _____ don't always win the race.

19. Sometimes, the boat tips over, and _____ land in the water.

20. Dad showed _____ how to right a boat that's capsized.

21. It's hard work, and it takes _____ a long time.

22. My sister laughs and waves as she sails past _____ .

23. _____ just grin and try to bear it.

24. After all, she did teach _____ how to swim!

 **Editing**  **Read Craig's last paragraph. Find and correct three personal pronouns that Craig misused.**

| Mistakes | | |
|---|---|---|
| | Capitalization | 2 |
| | Punctuation | 3 |
| | Spelling | 5 |

I realy like water sports. Next summer, my sister and me want to join a swiming team. She is really good at the backstroke, I like freestyle. One of my friends is on the town swim team and he said it was fun and his family likes to go to swim meats. My friend and me are the same age, and he likes to swim freestyle, too. We will probably compete in the same events. Mom and Dad sed they would take my sister and I to swim meets that are away from home. Lots of parents like to go to the swim meets. Their fun for the adults as well as for the kids!

# POSSESSIVE AND DEMONSTRATIVE PRONOUNS

## Become a Super Writer

Jeff and his classmates are writing about places that their ancestors came from.

> My grandparents came to America as adults. The country of their birth is Sweden. Sweden is called the "Land of the Midnight Sun." That is because the sun shines at midnight during the summer months.

Jeff used two possessive pronouns: *My* and *their*. He also used a demonstrative pronoun: *That*.

### Definition · Usage

A **possessive pronoun** shows ownership. It can come before a noun or replace a noun. **Demonstrative pronouns** identify specific people, places, or things. They take the place of nouns.

| POSSESSIVE PRONOUNS Before a Noun | | | |
|---|---|---|---|
| my | your | his | her |
| its | our | their | |

| POSSESSIVE PRONOUNS Replace a Noun | | | |
|---|---|---|---|
| mine | yours | his | hers |
| its | ours | theirs | |

| DEMONSTRATIVE PRONOUNS | |
|---|---|
| this | that |
| these | those |

## Your Turn

Circle the possessive or demonstrative pronouns and write them on the lines.

1. These are interesting facts you should know about Sweden.

2. This is a place where the sun does not set in June and July.

3. That means in winter the sun sometimes cannot be seen.

4. Sweden is a country in Europe, and its capital is Stockholm.

5. Swedes are proud that their country is the fourth largest in Europe.

6. Grandmother taught me to count her way—in Swedish.

**Write the boxed letters in the order they appear.**

7. Swedish word for *one*:  ___ ___ ___

8. Swedish word for *three*:  ___ ___ ___

Choose pronouns from the word banks to complete these sentences. The clues in parentheses will help you choose. Pronouns can be used more than once.

| DEMONSTRATIVE PRONOUNS | | | |
|---|---|---|---|
| this | these | that | those |

| POSSESSIVE PRONOUNS | | | | | |
|---|---|---|---|---|---|
| my | mine | our | ours | your | yours |
| his | her | hers | its | their | theirs |

9. Swedes are proud of accomplishments like _____ of the Swedish scientist Alfred Nobel. (demonstrative)

10. The yearly awards named after Alfred Nobel are _____ legacy. (possessive)

11. _____ are known all over the world as the Nobel Prizes. (demonstrative)

12. Stories about Pippi Longstocking may be _____ favorites. (possessive)

13. Swedes consider Pippi to be a national treasure of _____ . (possessive)

14. _____ is because she was created by a Swedish author. (demonstrative)

15. Swedes have many interesting traditions; Namnsdag, or Name's Day, is one of _____ . (demonstrative).

16. Swedes have first names, just as we do, and dates are assigned to _____ names. (possessive)

17. A girl can look on a Swedish calendar to see what date would be _____ to celebrate. (possessive)

18. Sweden is an interesting country; you may want to do some research to learn about _____ other traditions. (possessive)

( Editing )  Edit Jeff's ad for a trip to Sweden. Find and correct four mistakes in the use of possessive or demonstrative pronouns.

| Mistakes | |
|---|---|
| Capitalization | 4 |
| Spelling | 3 |

It's my pleasure to help you plan you winter holiday. Celebrate the season with a trip to Sweden. On santa lucia day, girls put on your traditional white robes, red sashes, and crowns of candels. They serve you coffee and Swedish pastrys. Tour swedish homes decorated for the holidays. The candles, apples, heart-shaped baskets, and straw ornaments are for you to enjoy. End yours trip by feesting at a smorgasbord. These is a meal you won't soon forget!

# REFLEXIVE PRONOUNS

## Become a Super Writer

Lena and her classmates are writing book reports. Lena chose to read *Stuart Little* by E. B. White. Here is how Lena started her report.

*Stuart Little* is a book you will surely enjoy. I loved this story! I even bought <u>myself</u> a copy of this book.

The word *myself* is a pronoun. It refers back to the subject *I*, which stands for *Lena*. Lena did not buy the book for a friend. She bought it for *herself*.

**Definition**

A **reflexive pronoun** reflects the action of the verb back to the noun that is the subject.

**REFLEXIVE PRONOUNS**

| | |
|---|---|
| myself | yourself |
| himself | herself |
| itself | ourselves |
| yourselves | themselves |

## Your Turn

**Circle the reflexive pronoun in each sentence. Then underline the subject that it reflects back to.**

1. Mr. and Mrs. Little surprised themselves with a son that looked like a mouse.

2. From the day he was born, Stuart could do a lot of things for himself.

3. Most babies can't walk by themselves, but Stuart could walk right away.

4. Stuart could shimmy himself up lamp cords when he was just a week old.

5. Mrs. Little was beside herself when she weighed one-month-old Stuart.

6. Stuart was able to feed himself, but he had gained just a third of an ounce.

7. Stuart helped his older brother, George, do things that he couldn't do himself.

8. When Mrs. Little's ring fell down the drain, she tried to fish it out herself.

9. Stuart said, "I'll help! I'll go down the drain and fish it out myself."

10. Mrs. Little agreed, but she warned Stuart to watch himself.

11. Stuart was so slimy after that trip that he took a bath and sprayed himself with Mrs. Little's violet water.

**Choose one of the words in parentheses to complete each sentence.**

12. One day, Stuart got up early and dressed (hisself, himself), as usual.

13. Mrs. Little's cat Snowball was in the living room, sunning (himself, myself).

14. As a rule, mice don't show (themselves, theirselves) when cats are around.

15. And Snowball, who was quite full of (hisself, himself), did not like Stuart.

16. Stuart started bragging to Snowball about how well he took care of (herself, himself).

17. To show off his stomach muscles, Stuart grabbed the window shade ring, meaning to pull (yourself, himself) up.

18. With a loud snap, the window shade rolled (itself, himself) up, dragging Stuart along with it.

19. When Snowball saw that Stuart was trapped, he just rolled over and said, "Now let me see you get (yourselves, yourself) out!"

 **Editing**  Help Lena edit the last paragraph of her book report. Find and correct three reflexive pronouns that are misused.

| Mistakes | |
|---|---|
| Punctuation | 3 |
| Spelling | 5 |

The best part of the book takes place in Central Park. Stuart managed to get itself to the park by takeing a bus. He went strait to the sailboat pond The pond was filled with boats. and Stuart wanted to go for a sail. A man agreed to let Stuart sail his boat, the *Wasp*, across the pond and back. Stuart ended up in a sailboat race. So many peopel came to wach the race that a policeman had to keep order. But the policeman got pushed and found hisself sitting in the pond. His fall caused a grate wave, which washed Stuart overboard? But Stuart pulled himself back onto the *Wasp* and won the race. I laughed myselves silly when I read this episode. You will, too!

# INTERROGATIVE PRONOUNS

## Become a Super Writer

Matt is writing a study guide to prepare for a science test on space travel.

*Who were the first astronauts? What does being in space do to you? Which mission took people to the moon? Whose space travelers are known as cosmonauts?*

Matt wrote four questions. He began each one with an interrogative pronoun. He used the pronoun *who* to ask about people. He used *what* and *which* to ask about things. He used *whose* to ask about ownership or possession.

**Usage**

An **interrogative pronoun** can be used to ask a question.

### INTERROGATIVE PRONOUNS

who     whom
what
which     whose

## Your Turn

**Underline the pronoun that correctly completes each question.**

1. _____ planet is closest to Earth?     Which (w)     Who (x)

2. _____ landed on the moon first?     Which (g)     Who (h)

3. _____ space station is in space now?     Whose (e)     Who (f)

4. _____ effect does space have on humans?     What (n)     Whose (o)

5. _____ set a record for days in space?     Whose (h)     Who (i)

6. _____ flag is planted on the moon?     Who (s)     Whose (t)

7. _____ do astronauts eat in space?     What (i)     Which (j)

8. _____ spacecraft is reusable?     Which (s)     Who (t)

9. _____ is it like on other planets?     Who (e)     What (f)

10. _____ planet did *Pathfinder* explore?     Which (u)     Whose (v)

11. _____ was the first human in space?     Who (l)     What (m)

12. _____ job involves space experiments?     Who (k)     Whose (l)

**To answer the riddle, write the letters that follow your underlined words, in order, on the lines provided.**

13. When can't you land on the moon?

___ ___ ___ ___ ___   ___ ___ ___ ___ ___   ___ ___

**Read each statement. Then write a question that might help you remember the information. Use interrogative pronouns.**

**14.** Yuri A. Gagarin, a Russian cosmonaut, was the first person in space.

_____

**15.** The first American to travel in space was Alan B. Shepard, Jr.

_____

**16.** Astronauts Kathryn Thornton and Eileen Collins were once Girl Scouts.

_____

**17.** The word *cosmonaut* means "universe sailor," while *astronaut* means "star sailor."

_____

**18.** The job of mission control specialists is to direct missions from the ground.

_____

**19.** Sally Ride was the youngest American astronaut to travel in space.

_____

**20.** The planet Mars is scheduled to be explored by robot probes.

_____

**21.** The asteroid belt is probably the next steppingstone after Mars.

_____

 **Editing** Here is more of Matt's study guide. Write an interrogative pronoun to complete each question.

| Mistakes | |
| --- | --- |
| Punctuation | 3 |
| Spelling | 4 |

_____ are the effects of spaceflight on an astronaut's body.

Almost half of all astronauts feel lightheaded and sick to their stomacks

during their first few days in space Their necks throb and there heads and

chests feel stuffed up.

_____ parts of an astronaut's body are affected by waitlessness!

Since gravity isn't compressing their spines, astronauts get a few inches

taller. Their bones lose calcium, and their muscles loose mass because they are

not working so hard.

NAME _____

# AGREEMENT WITH ANTECEDENT

## Become a Super Writer

Claire was writing a social studies report on the Battle of Antietam.

The <u>day</u> began peacefully in Sharpsburg, Maryland, but <u>it</u> would not end that way. <u>Robert E. Lee</u> wanted a victory in Union territory. <u>He</u> had invaded Maryland to win that victory. The <u>Confederates</u> didn't know <u>they</u> were about to be badly beaten.

In her opening sentences, Claire chose her pronouns carefully. She used the pronoun *it* to refer to the noun *day*. She used the pronoun *he* to refer to the noun *Robert E. Lee*. She used *they* to refer to *Confederates*.

### Definition · Usage

An **antecedent** is the noun to which a pronoun refers. A pronoun must agree with its antecedent. If, for example, the noun is singular, then the pronoun should also be singular. If the noun names a man, then the pronoun should be masculine.

## Your Turn

**Circle the pronouns in these sentences. Draw a line from each pronoun to the noun that is its antecedent.**

1. Lee's troops invaded Maryland, and they moved toward Pennsylvania.

2. President Lincoln summoned George McClellan and ordered him to stop Lee.

3. The two armies met at Antietam Creek, where they fought a battle.

4. The battle was bloody; in fact, it was the bloodiest of the Civil War.

5. More than 11,000 Union soldiers were either killed or they were wounded.

6. The Confederacy had fewer soldiers, but still it suffered about 9,000 casualties.

7. General Lee retreated to Virginia, but McClellan did not pursue him.

8. President Lincoln had won a victory, but it was not a decisive one.

9. On September 22, Lincoln read the Emancipation Proclamation to his Cabinet.

10. Speaking for African Americans, Frederick Douglass said, "We shout for joy that we live to record this righteous decree."

**Choose the pronoun in parentheses that correctly completes each sentence. Write the pronoun on the line.**

11. When Lee invaded Maryland, he had about 50,000 troops with _____ . (him, them, her)

12. Lee sent some of _____ men with General "Stonewall" Jackson to capture Harpers Ferry. (her, their, his)

13. During Jackson's march, an incident occurred, and John Greenleaf Whittier later wrote a poem about _____ . (him, it, them)

14. The poem is called "Barbara Fritchie," and _____ is about a woman who lived in Frederick, Maryland. (it, she, they)

15. The poem says that when Jackson rode through Frederick, _____ saw only one Union flag left flying. (it, he, they)

16. The flag belonged to Barbara Fritchie, and Jackson ordered his men to shoot _____ down. (it, them, him) it

17. Barbara Fritchie begged Jackson to spare the flag and to shoot _____ instead. (her, him, it)

18. Barbara Fritchie was ninety years old, but _____ wasn't afraid to anger the Confederate troops. (her, she, he)

19. Jackson ordered his troops to march on, and _____ did indeed spare Barbara Fritchie's flag. (them, she, they)

**Editing**   Edit this paragraph. Replace three pronouns that do not agree with their antecedents.

| Mistakes | |
| --- | --- |
| Punctuation | 1 |
| Spelling | 5 |

By sunset the Battle of Antietam was over. The armies of the North and South held about the same ground as it held at the start of the battle. More then 3,600 soldiers died and thowsands more were wounded in this battle. It was the bloodyest one-day battle in American history. Many historians say that niether side won a real victory at Antietam. However, them think it did help the Union in later battles. The Army of Northern Virginia lost one forth of his men, General Lee retreated to Virginia. Historians say the battle was a terning point in the war.

# PREPOSITIONS, PREPOSITIONAL PHRASES

## Become a Super Writer

Robert is writing an article about how to set up a home aquarium. He wrote:

*Having an aquarium has taught me a lot <u>about tropical fish.</u>*

Robert used a prepositional phrase in this sentence. The preposition *about* relates *tropical fish* to the word *taught*.

### Definitions

A **preposition** is a word that relates a noun or pronoun to another word in the sentence.

A **prepositional phrase** is a group of words that begins with a preposition and ends with a noun or a pronoun. Describing words may come in between.

### COMMON PREPOSITIONS

| | | | | | | |
|---|---|---|---|---|---|---|
| about | after | around | at | before | behind | beside |
| by | down | during | for | from | in | into |
| like | near | of | off | on | onto | out of |
| over | since | through | to | under | until | with |

## Your Turn

**Read each sentence. Underline the prepositional phrase, and circle the preposition.**

1. This article tells about home aquariums.

2. Aquariums can display many kinds of fish and plants.

3. You need some basic equipment for your home aquarium.

4. Begin your aquarium with these items.

5. You need a sturdy tank for the water.

6. You may want to put a cover on the tank.

7. Some covers have lights built into them.

8. You need a filter for purifying the water.

9. A heater will warm the water for the fish.

10. With this equipment, you can set up an aquarium.

**Add a prepositional phrase to each sentence, using the phrases in the word bank or your own. Write the new sentences. Circle the prepositions in them.**

| | | | |
|---|---|---|---|
| for the fish | through their gills | in the tank | with care |
| like other fish | at a pet shop | to live young | from the Caribbean |

11. Choose the fish for your aquarium.

_____

12. Buy food for your fish.

_____

13. Grow some water plants.

_____

14. Plants provide oxygen.

_____

15. Fish take oxygen from the water.

_____

16. Guppies are tropical fish.

_____

17. Guppies do not lay eggs.

_____

18. Guppies give birth.

_____

 **Editing** Edit the following paragraph. Fix five spelling mistakes in prepositional phrases.

| Mistakes | |
|---|---|
| Capitalization | 2 |

It's time to stock your aquarium. You may want to begin with just a few diffrent kinds of tropicle fish. Choose fish that do not fight with each udder. Guppies are among the easiest fish to raise. Also popular are tetras and angelfish. Tetras are among the most colorful of all fish. Neon tetras have brite blue stripes on the sides of their bodys. Angelfish also have stripes and patches of collir. They come from the Amazon river in brazil.

NAME _____

# OBJECT OF PREPOSITION

## Become a Super Writer

Jamie interviewed a local archaeologist. She wrote these notes.

Mr. Porter has been an archaeologist <u>for ten years</u>. An archaeologist uncovers what's left <u>of ancient cities and towns</u>.

Jamie used a prepositional phrase in each sentence. In the first sentence, the object of the preposition *for* is the noun *years*. In the second sentence, the object of the preposition *of* is *cities and towns*. Notice that it is a compound object. Also notice that both prepositional phrases contain adjectives that describe the nouns. *Ten* describes *years; ancient* describes *cities and towns*.

**Definition**

The **object of a preposition** is the noun or pronoun that follows the preposition. The object of a preposition can be one word, or it can be a compound.

## Your Turn

**Read these sentences. Circle each preposition, then underline the object of the preposition. One sentence has a compound object.**

1. The trilobite is an ancestor of crabs and lobsters.
2. Trilobites swam in the warm ocean waters.
3. The trilobite lived during the Paleozoic era.
4. At that time, trilobites were among the biggest animals.
5. They were only about one foot long.
6. Their hard-shelled bodies were divided by two deep furrows.
7. Archaeologists have found trilobite fossils in rocks.
8. Those rocks were once deep under the sea.
9. Pressures inside the earth pushed the rocks up.
10. After many years, the rocks were lifted to mountaintops.
11. It was on mountaintops that archaeologists found the fossils.

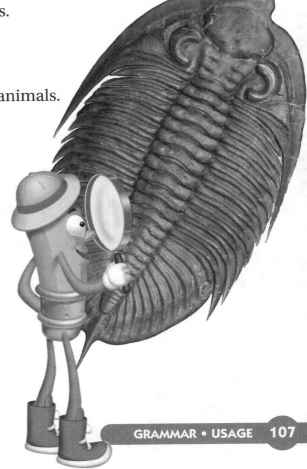

Find eight nouns in the word-search puzzle, and write them on the lines.

```
o d l q n s d k u y z a
d f m y i x m n w e k k
t o p l m o u n t a i n
c d q n a t d r y r j u
l s e d l a y e r s p s
t i m e s d f i h g m e
s l i l k b o t t o m y
o s e a d w u m r d y i
```

_____

_____

_____

_____

_____

_____

_____

_____

The object of the preposition is missing in each sentence. Use the words above to complete the sentences.

12. These fossils have been saved in rock for millions of _____.

13. Fossils are clues that tell what life was like in ancient _____.

14. Rocks that have fossils in them are usually formed from _____.

15. The rocks pile up and are arranged in _____.

16. The youngest fossils are found at the _____.

17. The oldest fossils are at the _____.

18. Some fossils were found at the top of a _____.

19. The mountain had been pushed up from the _____.

**Editing** Edit this paragraph that Jamie wrote. Find and correct five objects of prepositions that are misspelled.

| Mistakes | | |
|---|---|---|
| | Capitalization | 1 |
| | Punctuation | 2 |
| | Spelling | 8 |

The fossil record is a history of ancient live. It is like a giant jigsaw puzle. Half the peices are still missing, and others appear a few at a time These pieces give us a picture of what life on Erth was like long ago. Some plants and animals have disappeared. others, however, have been around for many yeres. Sharks, for example, have existed for millyuns of years, but have hardly changed at all. Is this a sign that some creetures adapt well to many environments. Most sientists think so, and so do I.

NAME _____

# COORDINATING CONJUNCTIONS

## Become a Super Writer

Lynne was writing a biography of Florence Nightingale. She wrote:

Florence Nightingale was born in Florence, Italy. Her parents named her for that city.

Lynne reread these sentences and decided to combine them. She used the coordinating conjunction *so* with a comma to create one longer sentence.

Florence Nightingale was born in Florence, Italy, <u>so</u> her parents named her for that city.

> **Usage**
> A **coordinating conjunction** joins two or more words, phrases, or simple sentences.

**COORDINATING CONJUNCTIONS**

| and | but | or | nor |
|-----|-----|-----|-----|
| for | so | yet | |

## Your Turn

**Find the coordinating conjunction in each sentence. Write it on the lines.**

1. Florence Nightingale didn't need to work, for she came from a wealthy family.

2. Nightingale knew she was meant to help the poor or sick.

3. Nightingale had a busy social life, but she never forgot her goal.

4. She studied nursing and became superintendent of hospitals in London.

5. During the Crimean War, Nightingale gathered some nurses and sailed to Istanbul.

6. The hospital conditions there were terrible, yet Nightingale would not give up.

7. The soldiers called her "Lady with the Lamp," for she walked miles every night to care for them.

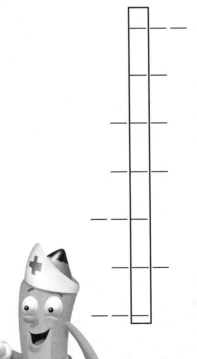

**Use the boxed letters to answer this riddle.**

8. What was Florence Nightingale to modern nursing?

   its __ __ __ __ __ __ __

**Choose a coordinating conjunction from the word bank to complete each sentence.**

> | but | or | for | yet |
> |-----|-----|-----|-----|
> | so | nor | and | |

9. The hospital in Istanbul had neither beds _____ bandages.

10. Nightingale found some healthy soldiers _____ put them to work.

11. She made schedules, planned diets, _____ cared for the sick.

12. Army officials resented Nightingale, _____ she was always asking for supplies they didn't have.

13. Nightingale would not put up with delays _____ carelessness.

14. The hospital was running well, _____ Nightingale eventually got what she wanted.

15. Nightingale caught Crimean fever on the front lines _____ nearly died.

16. The fever left Nightingale weak, _____ she never stopped working.

17. By the end of the war, she had saved many lives _____ had improved nursing.

 **Editing** The following billboard advertises Florence Nightingale's return from the war. Add three missing coordinating conjunctions.

| Mistakes | |
|----------|----|
| Spelling | 6 |

WELCOME!

Miss Florence Nightingale: The Lady With the Lamp

This frend of soljers risked life limb to help the injured. Now she is retterning to England to recover from her own ilness. Miss Nightingale is nearly an invalid, she plans to continue working. She wants to reform health care train nurses.

Join the party to celebrate her return. Mony collected will go toward a training school for nurses. Help reward this corageous young woman. Help make her dream come true. Attend the party atTown Hall, tonight at 7 o'clock. Admission is whatever you can afford.

# INTERJECTIONS

## Become a Super Writer

April wrote in her diary about her experience walking through the Sonoran Desert the very first time.

> Here I am in Arizona. I never thought I'd be able to get here. That was some view from the plane.

As April wrote, she realized she needed to include words and punctuation that described her feelings. She edited her first entry to include the interjections *Wow!*, *My goodness!*, and *Gee,*.

> <u>Wow!</u> Here I am in Arizona. <u>My goodness!</u> I never thought I'd be able to get here. <u>Gee,</u> that was some view from the plane.

### Definition · Usage

An **interjection** is a short exclamation that expresses a strong feeling.
- Use an exclamation point after a short interjection.
- Use a comma after an interjection that is part of a sentence.

## Your Turn

**Read these entries from April's diary. Circle each interjection.**

1. Well, here I am in the midst of the Sonoran Desert.

2. Oh, did I mention we are just a few miles north of the Mexican border?

3. Wow! This is the most unusual landscape I have ever seen.

4. The desert averages just eleven inches of rain each year. Imagine!

5. My! There are more plants and animals here than in any other American desert.

6. Look! It must have rained recently.

7. Those brightly colored flowers bloom only after rain. Wow!

8. Ouch! I pricked my finger on the spine of a cactus.

9. Well, next time I'll know better than to touch a spiny cactus.

10. Oops, I almost did it again.

**Find the interjections in the word search and write them on the lines below.**

_____  _____  _____

_____  _____  _____

_____  _____  _____

_____  _____  _____

_____  _____  _____

| | | | | | | | | |
|---|---|---|---|---|---|---|---|---|
| A | N | H | G | U | E | E | K | P | R |
| I | R | A | H | A | K | G | H | S | T |
| N | H | C | U | O | O | O | U | L | O |
| L | R | T | S | Q | O | O | R | T | L |
| E | O | H | H | P | L | D | R | K | L |
| R | L | I | S | T | E | N | A | M | E |
| D | K | O | O | P | S | P | H | E | W |
| R | W | H | E | W | K | W | O | W | O |

**Add an interjection to each sentence.**

11. _____ I see why they say the Sonoran Desert is so hot.

12. _____ Even the animals have learned to deal with the heat.

13. _____ there goes another lizard into hiding.

14. _____ There's a saguaro cactus.

15. _____ Is that a roll of thunder I just heard?

16. _____ This place needs some rain.

**Write two diary entries of your own that include interjections.**

17. _____

18. _____

**Editing** April wrote a paragraph that tells about plants of the Sonoran Desert. Underline the interjections she used.

| Mistakes | |
|---|---|
| Punctuation | 3 |
| Spelling | 6 |

Of course, cactuses are the champs of dessert plants. Ouch! Why are they so prickly. That's because their thick, spiney stems store lots of water after a rainstorm. The thick spines also shade and protect the stems. One type of cactus grows only in the Sonoran Desert It is the saguaro, the bigest cactus in the United States. Wait! Make sure you pronounce that sug-WAR-oh, or people who live there will laff. No kidding. Some saguaros grow up to fifty feet high. That's taller than a four-story bilding. They can weigh as much as an elefant.

# PRONOUNS, PREPOSITIONS, CONJUNCTIONS, INTERJECTIONS

**Review**

**Write a pronoun to complete each pair of sentences.**

1. John is a great athlete. _____ has been running since the age of five.

2. This medal was awarded to the winner. _____ is made of bronze.

3. The coach gave awards to several runners. John was one of _____ .

4. Certificates were also awarded. _____ went to all who participated.

5. One girl set a school record. _____ was very pleased and excited.

**Underline the pronouns that correctly complete these sentences.**

6. (I/Me) like to attend basketball camps.

7. The training makes (I/me) a better player.

8. I find it hard to practice by (himself/myself) sometimes.

9. The game (itself/themselves) requires a lot of energy.

10. You and your teammates must believe in (yourselves/yourself).

11. (Those/This) means you have trust in your abilities.

12. Perhaps you already knew (these/that).

13. (My/Mine) foul shot is almost as good as Pete's.

14. Last year it was the Jays' turn to win, but now it's (ours/ourself).

15. Matt did his favorite cheer, and then Darla did (she/hers).

16. Our voices were the loudest, but (them/theirs) were best.

17. (Who/Which) is the best player in camp?

18. (Which/Who) team will win the championship?

19. (Who/What) is the prize for winning the championship?

20. (Whose/Who) will award the prize?

**Circle each pronoun and underline its antecedent. Write _no_ if the two do not agree.**

21. The relay race will take place next, and it is for girls only. _____

22. Each runner must pass their baton to the next runner. _____

23. Marci ran with the baton but dropped it accidentally. _____

**Find the prepositional phrase in each sentence. Circle the preposition, and underline the object of the preposition.**

24. James Watt studied the kettle on the stove.

25. Steam arose from the kettle.

26. It was powerful enough to raise the lid off the kettle.

27. This gave Watt the idea for a steam engine.

28. He invented the steam engine in 1785.

29. It powered a whole factory of machines.

30. The power came from just one revolving shaft.

31. The power unit, the watt, is named for James Watt.

**Rewrite each pair of sentences as one sentence. Use one of these coordinating conjunctions: *and, but, or, nor, for, so, yet.***

32. The weather is sunny. The weather is warm.

   _____

33. I would play ball. Unfortunately I forgot my mitt.

   _____

34. Sam has an extra mitt. You can use his.

   _____

35. We all work hard. We still can't play well.

   _____

36. The boys didn't bring a bat. The girls didn't bring a bat.

   _____

37. Jim is playing in the outfield. Pat is playing in the outfield.

   _____

38. My sister will be pitching. I will be pitching.

   _____

**Underline the interjections.**

39. Ugh! I've walked another batter.

40. Whew! Ramon just struck out.

41. Wow! Kim just hit a home run.

42. Ouch! We're losing by four runs.

43. The bases are loaded. Hurrah!

44. Oops, there goes another game!

NAME _____

# PRONOUNS, PREPOSITIONS, CONJUNCTIONS, INTERJECTIONS

**Fill in the circle by the sentence that has a personal pronoun as the subject of the sentence.**

1. ○ He was a farmer.
   ○ The farmers shared their tractor.
   ○ During the summer, the farmers grew vegetables.

2. ○ Mike's class went to a theme park.
   ○ The school gave us free tickets.
   ○ We went together on a bus.

3. ○ Ms. Matthews is the track coach.
   ○ She ran track in college.
   ○ The whole team admires her.

4. ○ The children liked the spelling bee.
   ○ Mr. Bell held it the last day of school.
   ○ We had fun and won prizes.

**Fill in the circle by the pronoun that correctly completes the sentence.**

5. Would you like to play tennis with _____ ?
   ○ me       ○ he       ○ I       ○ we

6. _____ will serve the ball first.
   ○ Me       ○ Us       ○ Your       ○ I

7. For how long is _____ court reserved?
   ○ our       ○ him       ○ ours       ○ us

8. I will try to serve to _____ right side.
   ○ us       ○ you       ○ my       ○ your

9. _____ are the tennis balls we will use.
   ○ This       ○ That       ○ These       ○ It

10. Don't you think _____ is a fun game?
    ○ these       ○ they       ○ this       ○ those

11. Tennis is not a game you can play by _____ .
    ○ himself       ○ herself       ○ ourselves       ○ yourself

12. _____ sport do you prefer to play?
    ○ Who       ○ When       ○ Which       ○ Why

**Fill in the circle by the pronoun that agrees with the underlined antecedent.**

13. The <u>boys</u> met ____ troop for a camp-out at school.
    ○ his     ○ those     ○ that     ○ their

14. <u>Each</u> Boy Scout brought ____ own gear and supplies.
    ○ their     ○ our     ○ her     ○ his

15. <u>One</u> of the mothers said ____ would help with the food.
    ○ she     ○ her     ○ we     ○ they

16. The boys thanked the <u>woman</u> for ____ help.
    ○ she     ○ he     ○ her     ○ they

**Fill in the circle by the group of words that is a prepositional phrase.**

17. <u>The children</u>  <u>have put</u>  <u>their books</u>  <u>into their bags</u>.
    ○           ○           ○           ○

18. <u>The books</u>  <u>will stay</u>  <u>there unopened</u>  <u>until homework time</u>.
    ○           ○           ○           ○

**What kind of word is underlined in each sentence? Fill in the circle by your answer.**

19. <u>Imagine!</u> You can travel through some rain forests by boat.
    ○ pronoun     ○ interjection     ○ coordinating conjunction

20. Rain forests support many species, <u>yet</u> they are being cut down.
    ○ interjection     ○ coordinating conjunction     ○ preposition

21. Plants take in carbon dioxide <u>and</u> give off oxygen.
    ○ pronoun     ○ coordinating conjunction     ○ preposition

22. Plants release moisture into the <u>air</u> through their leaves.
    ○ pronoun     ○ preposition     ○ object of preposition

23. Plants soak up water from the soil with their <u>roots</u>.
    ○ interjection     ○ preposition     ○ object of preposition

24. Light and nutrients are needed <u>by</u> plants to grow well.
    ○ coordinating conjunction     ○ preposition     ○ object of interjection

# CAPITALIZATION, PART 1

## Become a Super Writer

Rosie wrote a report about Abraham Lincoln and discussed it with her teacher. Read these sentences from her report.

The president I admire most is Abraham Lincoln. He treated others as he wanted to be treated. For example, Lincoln said, "As I would not be a slave, so I would not be a master."

Notice how Rosie capitalized the first word in each sentence—*The, He, For.* She also capitalized the first word in the quotation, *As*, and the pronoun *I*.

**Rules**

Use a **capital** letter
- to begin the first word in a sentence
- to begin the first word in a direct quotation
- to begin the first word in dialogue or conversation
- to write the pronoun *I*

## Your Turn

**Read more about Lincoln from Rosie's report. Use the proofreaders' mark (≡) to show the words that should begin with capital letters.**

1. the sixteenth President of the United States was Abraham Lincoln.

2. he was born on February 12, 1809, in a log cabin in Kentucky.

3. "there was absolutely nothing to excite ambition for education," Lincoln recalled of his farming days.

4. Lincoln wrote about his education, "when i came of age i did not know much. still somehow i could read, write, and cipher."

5. altogether, his formal schooling totaled less than a year.

6. instead, Lincoln taught himself by reading books and newspapers he borrowed.

7. the young man studied law and became a lawyer in 1836.

8. twice, Lincoln was elected President.

9. lincoln once said, "a house divided against itself cannot stand."

10. rosie ended her report by writing, "he was a great man and served his country well. in my opinion, he was one of our strongest Presidents."

Abraham Lincoln often responded to questions with humor. Use the phrases below to create a dialogue between a reporter and Lincoln. Be sure to use proper capitalization.

Reporter: how long a man's legs should be

Lincoln: long enough to touch the floor

11. _____

12. _____

Reporter: any battles fought in the Black Hawk War

Lincoln: a good many bloody battles with mosquitoes

13. _____

14. _____

Reporter: a rival has called you two-faced

Lincoln: if I had another face, do you think I'd wear this one

15. _____

16. _____

**Editing**  Edit this paragraph from Rosie's report. Correct five mistakes in capitalization.

| Mistakes | |
|---|---|
| Punctuation | 2 |
| Spelling | 3 |

Abraham Lincoln's most famous speech was so short a photographer setting up his camera didnt have time to take a picture. the speech dedicated a battlefield in Gettysburg, Pennsylvania, as a cemetery for the soldiers who died there  Known as the Gettysburg Address, it begins, "four score and seven years ago our fathers brought forth on this continent, a knew nation, conceived in liberty, and dedicated to the proposition that all men are created ekwal." lincoln believed the Civil War was a test of these beliefs. he finished by saying, "this nation under God shall have a new birth of freedom—and that government of the poeple, by the people, for the people, shall not perish from the earth."

# CAPITALIZATION, PART 2

## Become a Super Writer

After visiting President Franklin Delano Roosevelt's home, John decided to write a biographical report about him. Read his opening sentences.

*Franklin Delano Roosevelt was born on January 30, 1882. He was America's thirty-second President. President Roosevelt, or F.D.R., led the United States through the Great Depression and World War II.*

Notice that John capitalized the proper nouns and proper adjectives in his sentences. He also capitalized the initials for Roosevelt's name.

**Rules**

Use a **capital** letter to begin proper nouns and adjectives, including
- words that name specific people, places, things, and events
- words that name days, months, and holidays
- words that show family relationships, such as *Uncle Teddy*
- words like *Mom* and *Dad* when they are used in place of proper nouns
- initials like *F.D.R.* and *UN*, for United Nations

## Your Turn

**Edit these sentences from John's report. Use the proofreaders' mark (≡) to correct the words that should begin with capital letters.**

1. Franklin and eleanor were married on march 17, saint patrick's day, 1905.

2. Five of their children were named anna eleanor, james, john, elliott, and franklin delano junior.

3. The family liked to visit campobello island, which is off the coast of new brunswick, canada.

4. roosevelt was there in 1921, when he caught polio.

5. roosevelt was partially paralyzed by the polio.

6. He was still able to serve as president of the u.s.

7. Roosevelt formed new programs and agencies to help america get through the great depression.

8. One agency was ccc (civilian conservation corps), which employed young people to perform public works, such as constructing public parks.

**Read these sentences. Underline the words that should be capitalized. Write them correctly on the lines.**

9. Franklin roosevelt was the only u.s. President to serve his nation for four terms.

   _____

10. Roosevelt was nominated to run for President in 1944 in chicago, illinois.

   _____

11. He ran against thomas e. dewey, a republican. _____

12. Roosevelt won the election and was inaugurated in january 1945; his Vice President was harry s. truman. _____

13. Roosevelt died the following april, just three months after his inauguration.

   _____

14. He had gone to warm springs, georgia, for a rest and was having his picture painted by elizabeth shoumatoff when he fell over at his desk.

   _____

15. After a funeral in washington, d.c., f.d.r. was buried at hyde park, new york.

   _____

16. Hyde Park is in dutchess county, on the east bank of the hudson river.

   _____

 **Editing** John also learned several interesting things about Eleanor Roosevelt. Help John edit this paragraph. Fix six errors in capitalization.

| Mistakes | |
|---|---|
| Punctuation | 2 |
| Spelling | 3 |

Eleanor's uncle, uncle Teddy, was Theodore roosevelt. He was the twenty-sixth President of the United states. Mrs. Roosevelt was the neice of one President and the wife of another. Eleanor Roosevelt also became famus in her own right. During World War II, she ran many activities for the Red cross. She worked hard to help people in need She gave lectures and wrote a dayly newspaper column. She became a delegate to the United nations. Eleanor Roosevelt was one of the most active first ladies in american history?

# CAPITALIZATION, PART 3

## Become a Super Writer

Naomi and her friends are putting together clue cards for a silly and serious trivia game. Here is one of the clues they have written.

*A Newbery Medal winner, this author wrote The View from Saturday. She also wrote a mystery about a girl named Claudia and a fascinating woman named Mrs. Basil E. Frankweiler. Who is the author?*

Notice that Naomi capitalized the first word and all the important words in the title of the book. She also capitalized *Mrs.*, which is a title of respect.

> **Rules**
>
> Use a **capital** letter to begin the first word and all important words in
> - titles of books, newspapers, magazines, headlines, plays, movies, and works of art
> - titles of stories, articles, poems, songs, and television shows
> - titles of people and of respect

## Your Turn

**The flip side of Naomi's trivia cards show the answers to the questions. Edit the answers. Use the proofreaders' mark (≡) to add capital letters as needed.**

1. In the movie *the wizard of oz*, dorothy must get help from a wizard.

2. *The lion king* is a movie and a play about a lion cub who becomes king.

3. Princess diana's full title was diana, princess of wales.

4. "The six o'clock evening news" comes on TV at six o'clock.

5. The poem "mary had a little lamb" tells about mary's little lamb.

6. *The new york times* is a newspaper published in new york.

7. *Sports illustrated for kids* is a sports magazine written for kids.

8. The national anthem of canada is "o canada!"

9. justice sandra day o'connor is a supreme court judge.

10. *dolphin sky*, by Ginny Rorby, is about a young girl and a pair of dolphins.

11. Washington, d.c., was named after president george washington.

**In the word-search puzzle, find and circle eight items whose titles require capitalization.**

```
D M A G A Z I N E
S O N G B P L A Y
T V S H O W A F E
O I J P O E M G L
R E C H K N B M R
Y I K W Y O T S P
```

**Write the words you circled above and give an example of each one.**

12. _____

13. _____

14. _____

15. _____

16. _____

17. _____

18. _____

19. _____

 **Editing**    Help Naomi edit these silly trivia questions. Fix six errors in capitalization.

| Mistakes | |
|---|---|
| Punctuation | 2 |
| Spelling | 5 |

1. Beethoven's <u>fifth Symphony</u> was written by what famus composer?

2. What legendary king is featured in <u>The Book of king Arthur and His Nights</u> by Mary McCleod?

3. In what sity is the newspaper <u>The Chicago Sun Times</u> published.

4. How many dalmatians appear in the movie <u>101 dalmatians</u>?

5. Henry Wadsworth Longfellow's pome "Paul Revere's ride" is about what Revolutionary War hero?

6. On the television show "Dr. Quinn, medicine Woman," what is Doctor Quinn's profession.

7. How often duz the news magazine <u>newsweek</u> come out?

# CAPITALIZATION, PART 4

## Become a Super Writer

Muhamed's family is spending two weeks in England. Read the first postcard he sent home to his cousin in Colorado.

Dear Ahmed,

We landed at Heathrow Airport, and then a cab drove us to our hotel in London. The driver was really nice. He took us by the lion in Trafalgar Square and by the Houses of Parliament to see Big Ben. We're off to visit the National Gallery right now!

Your cousin,

Muhamed

Mr. Ahmed Gabran

1124 Pitkin Street

Ft. Collins, CO 80237

U.S.A.

Notice the words Muhamed capitalized in the greeting and closing of his postcard. Look also at the place names he capitalized in the address and in the body of his message.

### Rules

Use a **capital** letter
- to begin place names such as streets, cities, and countries
- to begin the names of geographical features
- to begin the greeting and closing of a letter

## Your Turn

Capitalize the following names and write them in the correct columns.

laurel avenue
white mountains
austria
texas

the statue of liberty
lincoln memorial
lake ontario
elm terrace

thailand
florida
san francisco
pittsburgh

**Street**

1. _____

2. _____

**City**

5. _____

6. _____

**State**

9. _____

10. _____

**Country**

3. _____

4. _____

**Geographical Feature**

7. _____

8. _____

**Place**

11. _____

12. _____

**Write a letter asking for information on a place you'd like to visit.
Use Muhamed's letter below and the phrases in parentheses as a guide.
Remember to capitalize place names and letter parts as needed.**

13. (your name) _____

14. (street) _____

15. (city, state, zip) _____

16. (greeting)_____ ,

17. (request 1)_____

_____

18. (request 2)_____

_____

19. (closing)_____

20. (signature)_____

 **Editing** Help Muhamed edit his letter to a travel
agency. Fix six errors in capitalization.

| Mistakes | |
|---|---|
| Punctuation | 2 |
| Spelling | 4 |

Muhamed Patel

11 West end Avenue

Littleton, co 80120

Dear Sir or Madam:

    I wood like information on places to visit in and near London, England

I am interested in history and want to lirn more about places like the

tower of London and Windsor Castle. My sister is interested in finding out

abowt Westminster Abbey and Buckingham palace. My parents need

information about the Lake District and the Isle of wight in the English

Channel. Thank you for your help

                        sincerly yours,

                        Muhamed Patel

# CAPITALIZATION, PART 5

## Become a Super Writer

Suki wrote an outline for her report on dogs. Here is part of her outline.

Dogs (title)

I. Characteristics of dogs (main topic)

II. Types of dogs (main topic)

   A. Working dogs (subtopic)

   B. Sporting dogs (subtopic)

Notice how Suki organized her topics. Main topics follow Roman numerals. Subtopics are indented and follow capital letters. Suki also capitalized the first word in each topic and subtopic.

**Rules**

An **outline** organizes ideas into topics, subtopics, and details.
- Use Roman numerals (I., II., III.) to identify main topics.
- Use capital letters (A., B., C.) to identify subtopics.
- Use Arabic numerals (1., 2., 3.) to identify details.
- Capitalize the first word of each topic, subtopic, or detail.
- Indent subtopics and details to line up their numerals and letters.
- Include at least two topics or subtopics for each division.

## Your Turn

**Here is more of Suki's outline. Underline any words that should begin with capital letters. Circle any words that should not be capitalized.**

  II. Types of Dogs

    A. Working dogs

      1. Guard dogs

      2. sled dogs

      3. Rescue Dogs

    B. sporting dogs

      1. pointers

      2. Retrievers

      3. spaniels

**Write Roman numerals and capital letters to complete this outline. Then add another subtopic under "How to care for a puppy." Also add another main topic.**

So You Want a Puppy

_____ How to choose a puppy

    _____ Choose a puppy that fits your needs

    _____ Check the puppy's health

    _____ Test the puppy's temperament

_____ How to care for a puppy

    _____ Feed your puppy

    _____ Groom your puppy

    _____ Exercise with your puppy

    _____ _____

_____ _____

 **Editing**    **Suki added a third part to her outline. Edit the outline. Find and fix six errors in capitalization.**

| Mistakes | |
|---|---|
| Punctuation | 4 |
| Spelling | 2 |

III.    Famous dogs in histery

    A  Balto

        1.  eskimo sled dog

        2.  Carryed serum to fight diphtheria over 650 miles to Nome, alaska

    b.  Laika

        1.  first living thing sent into space

        2  Soviet scientists sent him up in a satellite in 1957

    C  leo

        1.  poodle saved owner from snake

        2  Received 1984 Dog of the Year Award

# CAPITALIZATION, PART 6

## Become a Super Writer

As part of a Girl Scout project, Becky wrote a report on the Red Cross. Read her introduction.

The Red Cross is a large organization that is found in almost every country in the world. But how did it begin? It started over one hundred years ago. A Swiss gentleman published a pamphlet in French during the Austro-Sardinian War in Italy.

Notice how Becky used capital letters to begin the names of an organization, a nationality, a language, and a historic event.

**Rules**

Use a **capital** letter to begin the names of organizations, languages, nationalities, and historic events.

## Your Turn

**Edit Becky's sentences by marking those words that should begin with capital letters. Use the proofreaders' mark (≡).**

1. Jean Henri Dunant, a swiss philanthropist, founded the red cross.

2. Dunant was in Italy during the austro-sardinian war in 1859.

3. He was shocked at how the wounded austrian and italian soldiers were suffering.

4. Dunant wrote about his experiences and suggested that countries organize volunteers to help during times of war.

5. People from 16 countries met in Geneva, Switzerland, and formed the international red cross.

6. Clara Barton was a nurse who cared for wounded soldiers during the American civil war.

7. In 1869 she went to Switzerland to help the wounded in the franco-prussian war.

8. She saw the good work that the international committee of the red cross was doing.

9. When Barton returned to the United States, she helped establish the american association of the red cross in 1881.

**Complete each sentence.**

10. The International Red Cross was founded in _____ .

11. Switzerland has three languages: German, Italian, and _____ .

12. The official language of the United States is _____ .

13. _____ is the official language of Mexico.

14. The people of the Netherlands speak _____ .

15. The people of Sweden speak _____ .

16. In Greece, people speak _____ .

17. No one speaks _____ today, although it was the language of the Roman Empire.

18. The people of many Arab nations speak _____ , which is also the name for the numerals we use.

**Search the puzzle to find and circle the words you wrote above.**

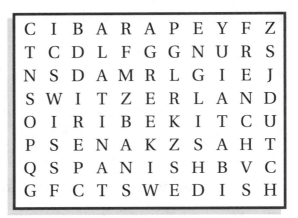

```
C I B A R A P E Y F Z
T C D L F G G N U R S
N S D A M R L G I E J
S W I T Z E R L A N D
O I R I B E K I T C U
P S E N A K Z S A H T
Q S P A N I S H B V C
G F C T S W E D I S H
```

 **Editing** Becky wrote a paragraph that tells how the Red Cross assists people in her community. Fix six errors in capitalization.

| Mistakes | |
|---|---|
| Punctuation | 2 |
| Spelling | 3 |

   Anyone kalling our local Red Cross chapter is not surprised to hear a message in both english and Spanish. You might even talk to a volunteer who speaks vietnamese. Our community has a big Hispanic and asian population. Being able to speek the different languages in a community is just one way the Red cross helps It helps groups like the junior league organize blood drives It also gives first-aid and watter-safety classes to various groups.

# ABBREVIATIONS

## Become a Super Writer

Bill wanted to order a model airplane he had seen advertised on television, but he never had enough time to get the address before the commercial was over. Finally, Bill got it—by using abbreviations.

Jan. to Dec. Designs, Inc.
P.O. Box 123
W. End Blvd.
NY, NY  10016

Bill used seven abbreviations: **Jan.** for *January,* **Dec.** for *December,* **Inc.** for *Incorporated,* **P.O.** for *Post Office,* **W.** for *West,* **Blvd.** for *Boulevard,* and **NY** for *New York.*

### Definition · Rules

An **abbreviation** is a shortened form of a title or some other word or phrase used to save time or space.

- Abbreviations begin with a capital letter and end with a period.
- For state names, the U.S. Postal Service uses two capital letters without periods.

> What did the letter carrier say to Hawaii and Massachusetts ?
> HI, MA !

## Your Turn

Write the abbreviations for the underlined words below.

1. Acme <u>Company</u> _____
2. <u>December</u> break _____
3. <u>Tuesday</u> morning _____
4. <u>Senator</u> Barkley _____
5. Park <u>Avenue</u> _____
6. <u>October</u> harvest _____
7. <u>North Carolina</u> _____
8. <u>Wednesday</u> special _____
9. the ides of <u>March</u> _____
10. Security <u>Corporation</u> _____
11. <u>Friday</u> the 13th _____
12. <u>Lieutenant</u> Juarez _____
13. <u>Doctor</u> Ames _____
14. River <u>Road</u> _____
15. Orlando, <u>Florida</u> _____
16. <u>Reverend</u> Smith _____
17. Toys <u>Incorporated</u> _____
18. Parks <u>Department</u> _____
19. Elm <u>Street</u> _____
20. <u>February</u> sales _____

**Complete the crossword puzzle by writing the full word or words for the underlined abbreviations. Use capitalization as needed.**

**Down**

1. <u>Mr.</u> Larsen is a filmmaker.

2. In <u>Aug.</u> he will be traveling.

3. His first trip is to Sacramento, <u>CA.</u>

4. He then goes to the <u>E.</u> Coast.

6. On <u>Tues.</u> he films a show.

8. After that, it's Madison <u>Ave.</u> in New York City.

**Across**

5. Next he heads to Hollywood, near <u>LA.</u>

7. Dover, <u>DE</u>, is his next stop.

9. His office is there at Reality Films <u>Corp.</u>

 **Editing** Bill made a few mistakes as he quickly jotted down telephone messages for family members. Fix five errors in capitalizing abbreviations.

| Mistakes | |
| --- | --- |
| Punctuation | 5 |
| Spelling | 2 |

Mom — Call dr. Parker for appointment on tues

— Grandma caled from her new Fl. apartment.

Dad — Pick up Carly from Tina's house, 11 River rd.

— Pictures are reedy at Park Ave Photo.

Carly — Can you baby-sit for mrs. Li on Sat. Mar. 5?

— Can you sell tickets at the school play on Fri. night.

# CAPITALIZATION AND ABBREVIATION

Review

**Edit the dialogue to fix the words that should begin with capital letters, using the proofreaders' mark (≡).**

1. "look at this poem," Ben said. "i think it's printed wrong."

2. "it must be by e. e. cummings," responded mom. "who's he?" Ben asked.

3. "a poet who ignored grammar and punctuation rules," mom said.

4. "it's all jumbled together and hard to read," commented Ben.

**Underline the proper nouns and adjectives that should be capitalized and write them correctly.**

5. In the u.s.a., thanksgiving is on the fourth thursday in november.

   _____

6. For my canadian cousins, it is the second monday in october.

   _____

7. We telephone montreal to speak with aunt andrea then.

   _____

**Capitalize these titles correctly. Write the titles on the lines.**

8. *national geographic world* (magazine)  _____

   _____

9. "rats outsmart scientists" (article)  _____

   _____

10. *mrs. frisby and the rats of NIMH* (book)  _____

    _____

11. principal ima mouse (person)  _____

**Capitalize the following names of historic events, organizations, languages, and nationalities correctly.**

12. the sons of liberty  _____

13. war for independence  _____

14. Some german soldiers knew no english but still helped the british.

    _____

    _____

**Use the information in the box to address an envelope to Summer Camps. Capitalize and add abbreviations as needed. Use your own address as the return address.**

mister sam adams president
summer camps, incorporated
104 concord street
somerville, va 23234

15. _____

16. _____

17. _____

18. _____

19. _____

20. _____

21. _____

**Here is a letter a student wrote to Summer Camps, Incorporated. Add the missing greeting and closing. Capitalize as needed.**

22. (greeting) _____

I am interested in attending camp this summer. Please send me information

about summer camps near Richmond, Virginia. Thank you for your time.

23. (closing) _____

24. (signature) _____

**Fix this outline. Capitalize, indent, and add punctuation.**

Trains                          25. _____

  I.  kinds of trains          26. _____

    A.  Freight trains        27. _____

    B.  Passenger Trains      28. _____

  II.  The railroad industry   29. _____

  A.  In the United States      30. _____

    B  In Canada              31. _____

    C.  in other Countries     32. _____

NAME _____

# CAPITALIZATION AND ABBREVIATION

**Read each sentence. Fill in the circle by the word that should be capitalized.**

1. Last night my brother, Mom, and i went to a ball game.

   ○ night          ○ i          ○ game

2. The announcer said, "please stand for our national anthem."

   ○ announcer      ○ please     ○ national

3. the crowd began to cheer, and the umpire yelled, "Play ball."

   ○ the            ○ crowd      ○ umpire

**Read the phrases. Fill in the circle by the proper nouns and adjectives that are capitalized correctly.**

4. ○ columbus day, the second Monday in October

   ○ Columbus Day, the second Monday in October

5. ○ Uncle Gomez              ○ uncle Gomez

6. ○ Martin Luther King, Jr.  ○ Martin Luther King, jr.

7. ○ T. s. eliot, the poet    ○ T. S. Eliot, the poet

8. ○ Memorial day weekend     ○ Memorial Day weekend

**Read the titles. Fill in the circle by the title that is capitalized correctly.**

9. person   ○ President Bill Clinton          ○ president Bill Clinton
10. book    ○ *Little House On The Prairie*   ○ *Little House on the Prairie*
11. song    ○ "Auld lang syne"                ○ "Auld Lang Syne"
12. headline ○ "Blizzard Hits the Northeast"  ○ "Blizzard hits the northeast"

**Fill in the circle by the place names that are capitalized correctly.**

13. ○ Lake Bluff, Illinois         ○ lake bluff, Illinois
14. ○ the great lakes              ○ the Great Lakes
15. ○ the united States of America ○ the United States of America
16. ○ Mexico City, Mexico          ○ Mexico city, Mexico

**Fill in the circle by the address that is written correctly.**

17. ○ Mr. Nikos Doukas    ○ Mr. Nikos doukas    ○ Mr. Nikos Doukas
    Boston, MA  02129    220 main Street    220 Main Street
    220 main street    Boston, MASS  02129    Boston, MA  02129

**Fill in the circle by the answer that shows the correct form of each letter part.**

18. Greeting    ○ Dear aunt Nancy,    ○ Dear Aunt Nancy,

19. Closing    ○ Your Niece,    ○ Your niece,

20. Signature    ○ Sophie Walker    ○ Sophie walker

**Fill in the circle by the answer that shows the correct abbreviation and capitalization for each item.**

21. ○ Gov. christine Whitman of N.J.    ○ Gov. Christine Whitman of NJ

22. ○ Rug Weavers, Inc., Sedona, AZ    ○ Rug Weavers, inc., Sedona, A.Z.

23. ○ wed., Augt. 26    ○ Wed., Aug. 26

**Fill in the circle by the outline that has the correct form and capitalization.**

24. ○ I.  The Solar System    ○ I.  The solar system

    A. The Sun and Moon    A. The sun and moon

    B. The Planets    B. The planets

    II. Our Neighboring Planets    II. Our neighboring planets

    C. Venus    A. Venus

    D. Mars    B. Mars

**Fill in the circle by the answer that shows the correct capitalization for each item.**

25. ○ My sister joined the International Jugglers association.

    ○ My sister joined the International Jugglers Association.

26. ○ My Grandfather fought in the Korean war.

    ○ My grandfather fought in the Korean War.

# INDENTION, PERIOD, QUESTION MARK, EXCLAMATION POINT

## Become a Super Writer

Leigh Ann wrote a science report on constellations. Read her introduction.

*Do you wonder about the stars? There are so many of them! People of ancient civilizations saw patterns in different groups of stars. Take a closer look. Can you see the shapes they saw?*

Notice how Leigh Ann **indented** the first line of her paragraph. She then used three end marks for her sentences: a **question mark** (**?**) for the interrogative sentences; an **exclamation point** (**!**) for the exclamatory sentence; and a **period** (**.**) for the declarative and imperative sentences.

**Rules**

- **Indent** the first line of a paragraph.
- Use a **period** (**.**) at the end of a statement or a command.
- Use a period after the Roman numerals and capital letters in outline parts.
- Use a **question mark** (**?**) at the end of a sentence that asks a question.
- Use an **exclamation point** (**!**) at the end of a sentence or phrase that shows strong feeling or excitement.

## Your Turn

Read these sentences from Leigh Ann's report. Punctuate each sentence with a period, an exclamation point, or a question mark.

1. Do you know what a constellation is ____
2. A constellation is a group of stars ____
3. In ancient times these stars were named after animals ____
4. The Big Dipper lies in the constellation Ursa Major ____
5. The word *ursa* means "bear" in Latin ____
6. Ursa Major points to the North Star ____
7. Find the two end stars in the bowl of the Big Dipper ____
8. Follow the line these stars make to find the North Star ____
9. Do you see a very bright star ____
10. That's the North Star ____

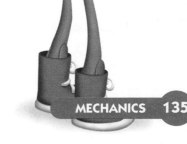

**Read each sentence. If the end punctuation is correct, write** *correct.* **If the end punctuation is incorrect, write the kind of end punctuation it should have.**

11. Orion, the Hunter, is an easy constellation to recognize? _____

12. Can you guess why Orion's easy to point out! _____

13. It's simple! _____

14. Look for three bright stars in a row. _____

15. These stars form Orion's belt? _____

16. Which constellation resembles a letter of the alphabet? _____

17. Why, it's Cassiopeia. _____

18. It looks like the letter "W" laying on its side. _____

19. What things do you see in the night sky. _____

20. Use your imagination and connect the stars. _____

 **Editing** Help Leigh Ann edit this paragraph of her report. Fix seven punctuation errors.

| Mistakes | |
|---|---|
| Capitalization | 4 |
| Spelling | 3 |

Cygnus is a bright, large constellation in the Northern hemisphere. It was one of the first constellations to be recognized and named Can you geuss what the word *cygnus* means in Latin? The english word *cygnet* is used to name a yung swan. Does that give you a clue. The word *cygnus* means "swan." That's just what Cygnus looks like?

people often told stories, or myths, about the constellations? One myth is about Cygnus. The myth says that Cygnus is in disguise. Cygnus is really Zeus, a Greek god. Another greek myth tells about Orpheus, a famos singer and harp player He was changed into a swan. Then he was placed in the night sky to be near his harp, the constellation Lyra.

# COMMA, PART 1

## Become a Super Writer

Angelo read *Dear Mr. Henshaw* by Beverly Cleary and liked it so much that he wrote a letter to his friend about the book.

398 Sommerville Ave.
Wilmont, KS 72943
February 19, 1999

Dear Greg,

We had to read <u>Dear Mr. Henshaw</u> for English class. I couldn't imagine liking a book with that title. But my teacher had said, "Honest, you'll love this book." She was right! Honest, you'll love it, too.

Your friend,
Angelo

Notice that Angelo used **commas** between the city and state and between the day and year. He also used a comma after the greeting and closing and before the quotation.

### Rules

A **comma** is used to keep words, phrases, and sentence parts from running together.
Use a comma
- to set off **cities from states** and **years from dates**
- after the **greeting** and **closing** of a **friendly letter**
- to set off a **direct quotation**

## Your Turn

**Add the missing commas to these sentences.**

1. Beverly Cleary was born in McMinnville Oregon on April 6 1916.

2. She lived on a farm in Yamhill until she was six, but then her family moved to Portland Oregon.

3. Beverly Cleary said about an essay contest she won when she was ten "I won two dollars, because no one else entered the contest."

4. She learned to be a librarian at the University of Washington in Seattle Washington.

5. This well-known author said "I simply write the books I wanted to read as a child."

6. One reviewer said about her book *Socks* "The story is clearly Cleary and great!"

**Write a letter to a friend about a book you've read. Include a direct quotation from the book or from the author.**

(address) _____

_____

(date)      _____

(greeting) _____

_____

_____

_____

_____

_____

(closing)      _____

(signature)      _____

 **Editing**    **Greg wrote back to Angelo. Edit his letter to fix four mistakes in punctuation with commas.**

| Mistakes | |
| --- | --- |
| Capitalization | 3 |
| Spelling | 3 |

35 Gravett avenue
Indianapolis IN 46290
June 20 1999

Dear angelo,

I went to borrow <u>Dear Mr. Henshaw</u> but it was already cheked out. I read <u>Strider</u> instead. It is a great book. Beverly Cleary has a good sense of humer. She also knows a lot about how kids feel. In his dairy, Leigh writes "I didn't care if that dog barked, bit, chewed up slippers, or chased cars, I loved him and somehow I had to keep him." I felt the same way when I found our dog banner.

Your pen pal
Greg

# Comma, Part 2

## Become a Super Writer

Read this paragraph from Sarah's science report on communication.

> Early people used drumbeats, smoke signals, and paintings to communicate with each other. People communicate differently today. Some people use the telephone, and others use the computer.

Notice that Sarah used **commas** to separate the items she listed. She also used a comma before the conjunction *and* to separate the two complete thoughts in a compound sentence.

**Rules**

In your writing, use a comma

- to separate items in a **series** or **list** of three or more things
- before a conjunction to separate two complete thoughts in a **compound sentence**

**Conjunctions**

and    or    but

## Your Turn

**Edit these sentences. Add the commas missing in the compound sentences and in the series of items in a sentence.**

1. Communication is very important and it is all around us.

2. Communication occurs at home school and work.

3. People communicate to share information and to show feelings.

4. Printing presses produce newspapers books and magazines.

5. Radios televisions telephones and computers connect us to the world.

6. Painting writing and gestures are also ways to communicate.

7. An artist uses color and a poet uses rhyme.

8. A smile shows happiness and a tear shows sadness.

**Read each sentence. If the sentence is a compound sentence, write**
*compound* **next to it. If it contains a series of items, write** *series.*

9. I use the radio, television, and computer every day.  _____

10. Radios, TVs, computers, and telephones can tell me
    about the weather.  _____

11. I enjoy watching television, but I prefer reading a good book.  _____

12. The parts of the newspaper I read include the comics, sports,
    and local news.  _____

13. I call my friends on the telephone, or I write them letters.  _____

14. Letters arrive in a week, but E-mail arrives in minutes.  _____

15. Every Monday, Wednesday, and Friday I E-mail my best friend.  _____

16. My granddad E-mails me once a month, and my aunt
    E-mails me on holidays.  _____

 **Editing**    Edit these paragraphs from Sarah's report. Fix
five errors in using commas. These errors are
counted in the punctuation mistakes.

| Mistakes | | |
|---|---|---|
| | Capitalization | 2 |
| | Punctuation | 7 |
| | Spelling | 3 |

   Telephones, televisions, and computers communicate information. All are

important forms of communication but they are not the only forms! Culor is often

used to share information. A red street light tells us to stop and a green one tells

us to go The colors of a neon sign capture our attention. bright orange yellow,

and red leaves hint that fall is just around the corner.

   We also use the names of colors to express feelings. A sad, lonely, or unhapy

person feels blue. a jealous person is green with envy and an angry one sees red.

Yelow is the sign of friendship. Colors help us to understand such things as maps

signs, art, and even people. They sure make the world more interesting?

# COMMA, PART 3

## Become a Super Writer

As part of career week, Steve went to work with his aunt. Read part of the summary he wrote of his visit.

> My aunt, Tracy Newman, is a newspaper reporter. Her day begins early each morning. First, Aunt Tracy goes to the newsroom. If she has any phone messages, she returns people's calls. For example, she called back a bank president who told her about a $10,000 donation to the library.

Steve used **commas** to set off a clause, an introductory word, and a phrase. He also used a comma to make a number easier to read.

**Rules**

In your writing, use a comma
- to set off **introductory words** and **phrases**
- to set off a **name in direct address**
- to set off **clauses**
- to make **numbers** easier to read (but not in years: 1999, 2001)

## Your Turn

**Read Steve's summary. Place commas where they are needed.**

1. While Aunt Tracy returns her calls I look around.

2. The newsroom the center of activity is very busy.

3. For example writers rush to prepare the day's stories.

4. First the reporters gather the news.

5. One reporter asks "Bob were you scared?"

6. While the reporter interviews Bob the photographer snaps a picture.

7. After the facts are collected the writer writes the story.

8. The writer prepares a story on Bob Hill a local firefighter.

9. Bob a real hero rescued a little girl.

10. Without a doubt I want to write for a newspaper!

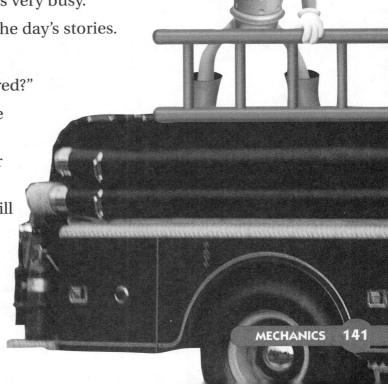

**Rewrite each sentence to show where commas should be added.**

11. The editor yelled "Tracy there's a three-alarm fire at 25 Oak Street."

_____

12. Without hesitating Aunt Tracy and I drove to the scene.

_____

13. Once we arrived Aunt Tracy scribbled notes into a notepad.

_____

14. After the fire was out she talked to the fire chief.

_____

15. "Thank you Chief. I'll call if I have any other questions" my aunt said.

_____

16. Before heading back to the newsroom Aunt Tracy made several calls.

_____

17. "Let's work fast Steve to print this story today!" she exclaimed.

_____

 **Editing** Read Aunt Tracy's newspaper story. Imagine you are her editor. Fix six places where commas are missing.

| Mistakes | |
|---|---|
| Capitalization | 2 |
| Punctuation | 6 |
| Spelling | 4 |

Earlier today, a fire destroyed a one-family home at 25 Oak Street. Within minutes the fire department was at the scene. According to the fire chief, a bad wire may have caused the blase. However Chief allen could not give us more informashon. He remarked, "Until we look into this matter we won't know what happened." He did tell reporters that the damage looked to be around $30000.

Vince Yates the owner of the home, was at work when the fire broke out. He was stunned by the loss. "ma'am I just can't believe it happened," he said. "Thankfuly, my family got out safely. That smoke detecter saved our lives!"

# APOSTROPHE

## Become a Super Writer

Shawn kept a diary while he was at summer camp. Read one of his sentences.

I saw four deer by the lake today. I <u>didn't</u> want to startle them, but I knocked one of the <u>canoe's</u> paddles into the water. The <u>deer's</u> heads went up, and then off they went. The <u>boys'</u> counselor saw what happened. He told me <u>we'll</u> see a lot more deer before the <u>summer's</u> over.

Notice how Shawn used **apostrophes** to replace the missing letters in the contractions *didn't* (*did + not*), *we'll* (*we + will*), and *summer's* (*summer + is*). He also used apostrophes to show possession for singular and plural nouns.

**Definition**

> An **apostrophe** signals letters that are missing in a contraction. It also signals ownership or possession.

| SINGULAR POSSESSIVE NOUN | PLURAL POSSESSIVE NOUN WITH *s* | PLURAL POSSESSIVE NOUN WITHOUT *s* |
|---|---|---|
| add an apostrophe +<u>s</u> | add just the apostrophe | add an apostrophe +<u>s</u> |

## Your Turn

Rewrite each phrase to create a possessive noun or a contraction. Be careful to use apostrophes correctly.

1. the shower will not _____

2. the cabins of the girls _____

3. the campfire of Friday night _____

4. the nest of the mice _____

5. the boys could not _____

6. they have bags of _____

7. the hoot of the owl _____

8. the flash of the lightning _____

9. the stories of the campers _____

10. you are on my _____

**Underline the words in each sentence that can be rewritten as a contraction or as a possessive noun. Then rewrite each sentence using these contractions and possessive nouns.**

11. At first, I did not know anyone in the dining hall of the camp.

    _____

12. The counselor of Cabin 5 called out the names of six campers.

    _____

13. You will never believe what the name of one camper was.

    _____

14. It is the same as mine, but the spelling of the name is different — S-E-A-N.

    _____

15. The little sister of Sean is at the camp of the juniors across the lake.

    _____

16. Can you believe she is also staying in the cabin belonging to my little sister!

    _____

 **Editing**    **Read part of Shawn's letter to his parents. Fix five errors in the use of apostrophes.**

| Mistakes | | |
|---|---|---|
| | Capitalization | 2 |
| | Punctuation | 2 |
| | Spelling | 3 |

All the cabins and the camps dining hall face the lake. The dining hall separates the boys cabins from the girls' cabins. Betwene the dining hall and the lake is Campers' Circle. That's where we meet for mail call, campfires, and news. Along the lake's edge is a sandy beach and a dock with canoes tyed to it. The canoes paddles, life jackets, and other equipment are stored in a shed by the lake.

Thats what camp looks like. now let me tell you about camp. I really didn't think Id like it, but I was wrong! It's terrific There are five other boys in my cabin. Their names are roshan, Jamie, Todd Benito, and Sam. You'll get to meet them when you come fore Parents' Weekend.

# QUOTATION MARKS

## Become a Super Writer

Sally's class had to create dialogues. Students were supposed to speak to writers from the past who were visiting the class with the help of a time machine. Read Sally's opening sentences:

"Mr. Ross, look at the time machine!" Sally exclaimed.

Mr. Ross looked at the flashing green light and said, "Yes, someone has come for a visit. Let's find out who it is."

Sally's dialogue uses **quotation marks** that show a speaker's exact words.

### Definitions · Usage

**Quotation marks** set off quotations and titles.
Use quotation marks

- before and after **a speaker's exact words** in dialogue, conversation, or direct quotations
- around the **titles** of **stories**, **poems**, **magazine articles**, **songs** and other short works

Periods and commas at the ends of quotations appear inside the closing quotation marks.

## Your Turn

**Read part of Sally's conversation with the brothers Grimm. Place quotation marks where they are needed.**

1. Well, if it isn't the Grimm brothers! Sally exclaimed.

2. Jakob grinned as he said, We prefer Brothers Grimm.

3. We don't like our name used as an adjective, Wilhelm added.

4. Sally nodded, That would make you appear a bit grim, wouldn't it?

5. We didn't create the stories, said Wilhelm. We wrote down the stories.

6. Jakob added, We gathered and translated old tales.

7. The brothers told German stories such as Hansel and Gretel.

8. They retold French and Italian tales such as Sleeping Beauty and Rapunzel.

**Rewrite these sentences from Sally's dialogue. Add quotation marks where they are needed.**

9. Do you know that many of your fairy tales are now movies? Sally asked.

   _____

10. What's a movie? Wilhelm whispered to his brother.

    _____

11. It's like watching a moving picture of the story, Jakob whispered back.

    _____

12. And to think that people didn't like our stories at first, Wilhelm sighed.

    _____

13. Sally gasped and said, They didn't?

    _____

14. Yes, they thought the stories were dull, Wilhelm said.

    _____

15. Jakob continued, We rewrote them using more colorful language.

    _____

16. Wilhelm nodded and said, We also made the dialogue more natural.

    _____

 **Editing**   **Sally wrote this paragraph to list some fairy-tale characteristics. Find and fix three places where quotation marks are needed.**

| Mistakes | |
|---|---|
| Capitalization | 2 |
| Punctuation | 2 |
| Spelling | 2 |

Fairy tales often begin with "Once upon a time" or Long, long ago." Good and bad characters usually appear in the same story For example, in Snow White," the bad queen tries to get rid of Snow white, but the good characters, the seven dwarfs, save her. The number three is important in many fairy tails. In Three Billy goats Gruff," there are three billy goats and three attempts to cross a troll's bridge Another very well-known thing about ferry tales is the way they end. Does the sentence "And they lived happily ever after" sound familiar?

# Underline, Italics, Colon, Hyphen, Parentheses

## Become a Super Writer

Mark's classmates worked together to write a play. Here's its beginning.

<u>Rumplestilts: A Modern Tale</u>

NARRATOR: (*Loudly*) In a small town about twenty-five miles from a big city, there lived a bank teller who had a beautiful daughter, Dawn. From 9:00 A.M. to 5:00 P.M., all the teller did was roll coins into paper wrappers.

Notice how Mark's class **underlined** the title of the play. They also used several punctuation marks: **colons (:)**, **hyphens (-)**, and **parentheses ( )**.

**Rules**

- Use **italics** or **underline** the titles of plays, books, movies, TV programs, magazines, and newspapers. Underline is used with handwriting, and italics with word processing.
- **Italics** are also used to show instructions in a play.
- Use a **colon** to show the speaking character in a play, to show time, to introduce a list of items, and after the greeting in a business letter.
- Use a **hyphen** between compound numbers, some compound words, and to divide words into word parts at the ends of lines.
- Use **parentheses** to set off instructions in a play or words that interrupt the flow of a sentence, or to explain something within a sentence.

## Your Turn

**Read more of the play. Add hyphens, colons, and parentheses where they are needed.**

1. TELLER (*Boasting* My daughter, who is only ten years old, could count and wrap all the bank's coins in one night.

2. BANK PRESIDENT: *Passing by*) If she can't, you're fired.

3. DAWN (*Sitting before a mountain of coins* What am I to do?

4. RUMPLESTILTS: *Appearing from thin air*) I can help. But you must promise to marry me when you turn twenty one.

5. DAWN (*Gratefully*) I'll do it to save my father's job, you odd little man.

6. TELLER *Admiringly*) My sweet, sweet child.

**Rewrite the following titles and phrases. Underline and use hyphens, colons, and parentheses where needed.**

**7.** topsy turvy   _____

**8.** ninety nine cents   _____

**9.** 230 in the afternoon   _____

**10.** Dear Sir or Madam   _____

**11.** the book Cinderella   _____

**12.** Newsweek magazine   _____

**13.** I wake up at 715.   _____

**14.** My uncle is a DJ disc jockey.   _____

**15.** the movie Beauty and the Beast   _____

**16.** Giant Angrily Fee, fie, foe.   _____

**17.** thirty one   _____

 **Editing**   **Read the ending to the play. Fix ten places where underline, italics, hyphens, colons, or parentheses are needed.**

| Mistakes | |
| --- | --- |
| Capitalization | 2 |
| Spelling | 3 |

NARRATOR: Dawn saved her father's job. Eleven years later, when she turned

twenty one, Dawn was to marry the bank president. But who arrived while

Dawn was reading Modern Bride magazine? That's right, the odd little man

who had wrapped the coins for her.

RUMPLESTILTS (Slyly) Hello, Dawn, my future bride.

dAWN: (Frightened) Oh, please. Release me from this promise.

RUMPLESTILTS:  I give you three days to guess my name. If you can't guess it by

1200 noon of the third day, you merry me. (Disappears in puff of smoke.)

DAWN: (Crying) Oh no, what's to become of me?

JANITOR: (Putting a hand on Dawn's shoulder Never fear. I herd the man singing

his name one nite. It is rumplestilts.

# PUNCTUATION

Add the correct end punctuation to each sentence.

1. What a surprise _____

2. Is that the right answer _____

3. Her dog is black and white _____

4. Wow _____

5. Answer the phone _____

6. Will the play start on time _____

7. He rode his bike to school _____

8. Close the window _____

**Write the following dates, addresses, direct quotations, and letter parts. Add commas where they are needed.**

9. December 7 1941 _____

10. Boston Massachusetts _____

11. Dear Phil _____

12. Mom said "Eat your lunch." _____

13. July 4 1776 _____

14. Topeka Kansas _____

15. Your friend _____

16. "Turn right" Susan said. _____

**Add commas to punctuate the compound sentences and the words in a series.**

17. Dad hoed the garden and it was now ready for planting.

18. We plan to grow corn green beans tomatoes and lettuce.

19. John wanted to begin planting the seeds but it started to rain.

20. Dad said it would be too wet to plant now and Mom agreed.

21. Then Mom set out an empty egg carton potting soil and tomato seeds.

22. The plan was to start the tomatoes let them grow a little and then transplant them.

**Place commas after introductory words, phrases, and clauses, in numbers, and in direct address.**

**23.** "Maggie did you see Bob's new telescope?"

**24.** Naturally he spends a lot of time looking at the moon.

**25.** Since it is a full moon everyone wants to look in the telescope.

**26.** The moon is about 240000 miles from the earth.

**27.** "May I have the telescope next Tina?"

**28.** "Thank you Adam for letting me look."

**Rewrite each group of words to create a contraction or a possessive noun. Be sure to use apostrophes correctly.**

**29.** the name of the princess _____

**30.** we have not seen _____

**31.** the scissors of the barbers _____

**32.** does not understand _____

**33.** the red car of Ms. Jenson _____

**Add quotation marks to the dialogue, quotations, and titles.**

**34.** Do you know how the elephant got a long trunk? Tom asked.

**35.** I have a book of tell-me-why stories that might help, said Mel.

**36.** The boys read The Town Without Taste, a silly short story.

**37.** They laughed over lines like marshmallow bread with dandelion butter.

**38.** Another story they liked was How the Leopard Got His Spots.

**Rewrite the following. Add underline or italics, colons, hyphens, and parentheses as needed.**

**39.** We get the New York Post. _____

**40.** The book is called Charlotte's Web. _____

**41.** The time is 430. _____

**42.** Wolf Roughly Let me in! _____

**43.** Little Pig (Loudly) No! No! _____

**44.** I have twenty seven pennies. _____

NAME _____

# PUNCTUATION

**Fill in the circle by the correct end punctuation for each sentence.**

1. It was a bright, sunny day
   ○ period   ○ exclamation point

2. Do you want to know a secret
   ○ period   ○ question mark

3. Ouch, that hurts
   ○ period   ○ exclamation point

4. Close the door, please
   ○ period   ○ question mark

**Fill in the circle to choose the correct use of commas.**

5. ○ January, 31 1992
   ○ January 31, 1992

6. ○ Dear, Jane
   ○ Dear Jane,

7. ○ Taos, New Mexico
   ○ Taos New, Mexico

8. ○ Sincerely yours,
   ○ Sincerely, yours

9. ○ Dentists say, "Brush daily."
   ○ Dentists, say "Brush daily."

**Fill in the circle by the sentence that uses commas correctly in compound sentences or in a series.**

10. ○ He likes math, but he dislikes science.
    ○ He likes math but, he dislikes science.

11. ○ Do you like softball or, do you like tennis?
    ○ Do you like softball, or do you like tennis?

12. ○ The train stops in Boston, New, York, and Philadelphia.
    ○ The train stops in Boston, New York, and Philadelphia.

**Fill in the circle by the sentence that correctly uses commas with introductory words, phrases, clauses, direct address, or numbers.**

13. ○ Well, that was a good movie.
    ○ Well that was a good movie.

14. ○ "Thank you Dave," Mona, said.
    ○ "Thank you, Dave," Mona said.

15. ○ They live 15,00 miles away.
    ○ They live 1,500 miles away.

16. ○ When I was late, Dad, got worried.
    ○ When I was late, Dad got worried.

**Read each sentence or phrase. Fill in the circle by the correct contraction or possessive form for the underlined words.**

**17.** We <u>will not</u> be able to go.   ○ wouldn't   ○ won't

**18.** <u>the sister of my mother</u>   ○ my sister's mother   ○ my mother's sister

**19.** <u>They have</u> too many books.   ○ They're   ○ They've

**20.** <u>the teacher of the children</u>   ○ the childrens' teacher   ○ the children's teacher

**Fill in the circle by the sentence that uses quotation marks correctly.**

**21.** ○ "The Walrus and the Carpenter" is a poem by Lewis Carroll.

   ○ "The Walrus" and "the Carpenter" is a poem by Lewis Carroll.

**22.** ○ "Is the poem funny? she asked." "Yes, very, he answered."

   ○ "Is the poem funny?" she asked. "Yes, very," he answered.

**23.** ○ Carroll wrote, "The sea was as wet as wet could be."

   ○ Carroll wrote, The sea was as wet as wet could be."

**Fill in the circle to choose the correct use of underline, italics, colons, hyphens, and parentheses.**

**24.** ○ I'm reading a book called "Twenty-One Instant Mysteries."

   ○ I'm reading a book called *Twenty-One Instant Mysteries*.

**25.** ○ One story (my favorite) is about buried treasure.

   ○ (One story) my favorite is about buried treasure.

**26.** ○ A news story about the treasure appears in the *Chicago Tribune*.

   ○ A news story about the treasure appears in the *Chicago* Tribune.

**27.** ○ The paper goes on sale promptly at 60,7 every morning.

   ○ The paper goes on sale promptly at 6:07 every morning.

**28.** ○ A panic follows and fifty six-people are injured.

   ○ A panic follows and fifty-six people are injured.

**29.** ○ The next day the paper prints a retraction that starts "Dear Readers:"

   ○ The next day the paper prints a retraction that starts "Dear Readers-"

# Syllables

## Become a Super Writer

Matthew is writing about Independence Day celebrations. He wrote:

*How do you celebrate the Fourth of July? Does your mom <u>fix</u> a <u>picnic</u> lunch for the family? Do you <u>take</u> part in a holiday <u>parade</u>?*

The word *fix* has a consonant-vowel-consonant pattern. The word *picnic* has this same pattern in each **syllable**. The word *take* has a consonant-vowel-consonant-final *e* pattern. The word *parade* has this same pattern in the second syllable. Thinking about patterns in syllables can help you spell words.

### Definition · Rules

A **syllable** is a word or part of a word. Each syllable has a single vowel sound. A **closed syllable** ends in one or more consonants. An **open syllable** ends in a long vowel sound.

- If a two-syllable word has two consonants in the middle, divide between the two consonants. (*pen • cil*)
- If a two-syllable word's first syllable has a long vowel sound, divide after the first vowel. (*spi • der*)
- If a two-syllable word's first syllable has a short vowel sound, divide after the middle consonant. (*tim • id*)

## Your Turn

**Read these sentences. Circle the two-syllable words, then divide the words into syllables. One word is a compound word. Divide it between the individual words.**

1. My friend, Steven, was the drum major for the band at the

   Independence Day celebration. _____

2. My dad planned the menu for our picnic lunch. _____

3. My mom cut up tomatoes for the salad. _____

4. I brought the plates, but I forgot the plastic forks! _____

5. I ate frozen yogurt for dessert. _____

6. I want to impress my friends by winning the three-legged race.

   _____

7. After dark, our town has a wonderful fireworks show. _____

**Divide the following words into syllables. Then write the words in the correct boxes below.**

8. common _____

9. moment _____

10. happen _____

11. medal _____

12. dragon _____

13. tariff _____

14. manage _____

15. hero _____

16. silent _____

17. capture _____

18. hotel _____

19. advice _____

20. whisper _____

21. model _____

22. basic _____

| Divide Between Two Consonants | Divide After First Vowel | Divide After Middle Consonant |
|---|---|---|
| _____ | _____ | _____ |
| _____ | _____ | _____ |
| _____ | _____ | _____ |
| _____ | _____ | _____ |
| _____ | _____ | _____ |

**Editing** Edit this paragraph. Correct five spelling mistakes in two-syllable words.

| Mistakes | |
|---|---|
| Capitalization | 6 |
| Punctuation | 2 |

The people of Mexico celebrate their independence on september 16. Long ago, on september 15, a priest in the villij of Dolores rang the bells of his church to summen the people. The priest, Padre hidalgo, wanted to break away from Spannish rule. He told the people to form their own goverment. This was the start of the mexican Revolution. Padre Hidalgo did not live to see his cuntry become independent but the people of Mexico still honnor him. On September 15 the president of mexico rings a bell in Mexico City. On September 16, there are parades and fireworks, just as there are in the United States on July 4.

# ENDINGS s, es, ed, ing

## Become a Super Writer

Martina wrote about learning to input text on a computer. She wrote:

*I am <u>begining</u> to learn to type. <u>Typeing</u> on a computer is fun!*

When Martina reread her sentences, she realized she made two spelling mistakes. She revised her sentences.

*I am <u>beginning</u> to learn to type. <u>Typing</u> on a computer is fun!*

**Rules**

If a verb ends

- with a short vowel and consonant, **double the consonant** when adding *ed* or *ing*
- with a consonant-*e* pattern, **drop the final e** before adding *es, ed,* or *ing*
- with two consonants, such as *lp, nt, rt, st,* or *nk,* add *s, ed,* or *ing* with no change in spelling
- in *ss, sh, ch, x,* or *zz,* add *es, ed,* or *ing* with **no change in spelling**

> **DOUBLE FINAL CONSONANT**
> bat: batted, batting
> wrap: wrapped, wrapping
>
> **DROP FINAL E**
> move: moves, moved, moving
> slice: slices, sliced, slicing
>
> **NO CHANGE IN SPELLING**
> start: starts, started, starting
> crash: crashes, crashed, crashing
> touch: touches, touched, touching

## Your Turn

**Read each sentence. Add the correct ending to the underlined word. Choose from *es, ed,* or *ing*. Write the new word on the line.**

1. I am always <u>hit</u> the wrong keys. _____
2. That's because I am <u>use</u> the wrong fingers. _____
3. My mother <u>teach</u> computer skills at my school. _____
4. She points out that I've <u>type</u> the wrong letters. _____
5. Yesterday, Colin <u>brag</u> about being a good typist. _____
6. I am <u>practice</u> so that I can improve. _____
7. <u>Type</u> is a very useful skill to have. _____
8. I'm glad Mom is <u>let</u> me use her computer. _____
9. <u>Write</u> is fun with word-processing software. _____

**Help Martina spell the following words correctly by adding the endings shown. Then use four of the words in your own sentences.**

10. stun + ed = _____

11. wave + es = _____

12. click + s = _____

13. swim + ing = _____

14. hope + ed = _____

15. jog + ing = _____

16. wish + es = _____

17. watch + es = _____

18. hug + ed = _____

19. care + ing = _____

20. hope + ing = _____

21. grab + ed = _____

22. start + ing = _____

23. blame + ed = _____

24. _____

25. _____

26. _____

27. _____

**Editing** Read what Martina wrote about typewriters. Correct seven spelling mistakes in verbs with the endings *es*, *ed*, and *ing*.

| Mistakes | |
|---|---|
| Capitalization | 3 |
| Punctuation | 2 |

The first patent for a typewriter was issued in 1714. This typewriter was not well planed, however. Writeing by hand was easier than trying to use this clumsy machine. In 1868, a really useful typewriter was invented. A few years later, e. remington and Sons startted selling it to the public.

Many businesses bought the new typewriters. Still, figureing out the best way to type on them was a problem Then someone introduced "touch typing." Typists learned to keep their fingers on the "home row keys." They used their thumbs for spaces between words.

The first electric typewriter appeared in the 1920s Sixty years later, people were tradeing in their typewriters for Computers. Moving words and sentences around is easy on a computer. Deleteing mistakes is a breeze!

NAME _____

# ENDINGS s, es, ed, er, ing

## Become a Super Writer

Dan wrote a report on his favorite pastimes. Read his first sentence.

*I have several hobbies. My favorite hobby is philately, or stamp-collecting. I also enjoy gardening.*

Notice that when Dan wrote the plural form of *hobby*, he **changed the final y to an i** before he added *es*.

**Rules**

If a word ends with
- a consonant + *y*, **change the y to i** before adding *er, es,* or *ed* and keep the *y* when adding *ing*
- a vowel + *y*, **simply add the ending**

### Y WORDS
carry: carries, carried, carrying, carrier
hurry: hurries, hurried, hurrying, hurrier

### VOWEL + Y WORDS
obey: obeys, obeyed, obeying
monkey: monkeys, monkeyed, monkeying

## Your Turn

**Use the clues to solve this crossword puzzle.**

**Across**

2. activities you do for fun
3. the plural of *lily*
4. to be making an effort to do something
5. the past tense of *survey*
7. the past tense of a verb meaning "to rush"
8. the past tense of a verb meaning "to answer someone"
10. the plural of *pansy*

**Down**

1. another word for *talents*
2. more happy
6. more than one variety
9. the past tense of *dry*

© MCP. All rights reserved. Copying strictly prohibited.

**SPELLING 157**

**"Add" these words and their endings to make new words. Write each new word on the line.**

11. valley + s = _____

12. envy + ed = _____

13. bury + ing = _____

14. country + s = _____

15. turkey + s = _____

16. noisy + er = _____

17. dry + ed = _____

18. journey + s = _____

19. marry + ing = _____

20. supply + er = _____

21. deny + ed = _____

22. duty + es = _____

**Find each new word in this puzzle and circle it.**

```
D E K C V A L L E Y S N
U L J O U R N E Y S R O
T E S U P P L I E R E I
I N O N B U R Y I N G S
E R R T U R K E Y S R I
S M A R R Y I N G R A E
O D R I E D Z E B N O R
M E D E N I E D O T S O
N Y R S A E N V I E D E
```

**Editing**  Read what Dan wrote about stamp-collecting. Correct six spelling mistakes in words ending with *y* and *ey*.

| Mistakes | |
|---|---|
| Capitalization | 4 |
| Punctuation | 2 |

    People all over the world use stamps as a way of paying postage. A philatelist, or stamp collector trys to buy as many rare stamps as possible. A Philatelist studys a stamp's paper, ink, printing process, and History. There are many varietys of stamps and many reasons for collecting them. Some people collect stamps of a single color or country. Others collect stamps with flowers ships, or trains. Specialtys vary widely. Right now my specialty is collecting stamps with birds. I even have some with pictures of turkeyes on them! uncle bob is my best supplyer of stamps.

# PREFIXES im, in, mis, non, pre, re, un

## Become a Super Writer

Nancy is writing a report on the rain forests. She wrote:

*The topic of my report is the rain forests. We need to be careful about how we use our natural resources. We must not misuse them. Sometimes, the damage we do to nature cannot be undone.*

Look at each underlined word. Can you find the **prefix** it begins with?

### Definition · Rules

A **prefix** is a word part added to the beginning of a base word or a root.

- When a prefix is added, a new word is formed that has a new meaning.
- The spelling of the base word is not changed when a prefix is added.

| PREFIX | MEANING | EXAMPLE |
|--------|---------|---------|
| im | not, opposite of | improper |
| | in, into | impress |
| in | not, opposite of | inactive |
| mis | wrong | misspell |
| non | not, opposite of | nonsense |
| pre | before | preheat |
| re | again | reread |
| | back | review |
| un | not, opposite of | unafraid |
| | absence of | untie |

## Your Turn

**Write a word with a prefix to complete each sentence. Use the clues in parentheses to help you figure out what word to write.**

1. This _____ book provides a lot of information about ecology. (not + *fiction*)

2. Unfortunately, the book is not _____ . (not + *expensive*)

3. There is a chapter on how to _____ paper and other products. (again + *cycle*)

4. There is also a chapter on _____ trees that have been cut down in forests. (back + *placing*)

5. The book points out how we have been _____ our natural resources. (wrong + *using*)

6. The earth's supply of natural resources is not _____ . (opposite of + *limited*).

7. You can find ways to _____ things instead of throwing them out. (again + *use*)

**Use the clues to complete the puzzle.**

Across

2. not living
7. to cook beforehand
8. to place wrongly
9. not perfect

Down

1. not direct
3. to print into
4. to pay back

5. to build again
6. not like

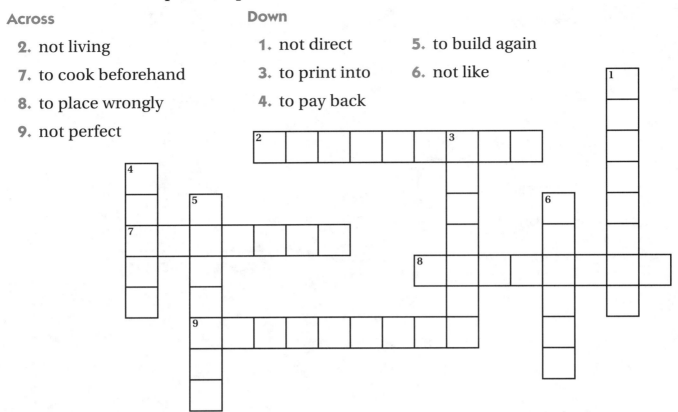

**Editing**   Read Nancy's paragraph. Correct the spelling of six words with prefixes.

| Mistakes | |
|---|---|
| Capitalization | 2 |
| Punctuation | 2 |

Many inusual plants and animals live in tropical rain forests. When trees are cut down and removed, animals lose their homes. Some may flee from the forests and never reapear. Some species may even become extinct. When we cut down trees, we do animals a great injustiss. There may be other unnown consequences, too. Many Scientists say that our earth is warming. Is this warming a result of the loss of our tropical rain forests. Some scientists think so?

Some people say that the scientists are reakting too strongly. Maybe these people misunderstand how Nature works. If you distreat nature in one place, I think other places will be affected, too.

# PREFIXES de, dis, ex

## Become a Super Writer

Brian is writing a narrative about his first camping trip. He wrote:

*I wished I could <u>exchange</u> places with my cousin. But I didn't want Uncle Jim to <u>discover</u> that I'd never been camping.*

Brian used two words with **prefixes**. Can you find the two prefixes?

---

**Definition · Rules**

A **prefix** is a word part added to the beginning of a base word or root.

• When a prefix is added, a new word is formed that has a new meaning.

• The spelling of the base word is not changed when a prefix is added.

| PREFIX | MEANING | EXAMPLE |
|---|---|---|
| de | undo | decode, defrost |
| | remove from | debug |
| dis | not, opposite of | dishonest |
| | lack of | discomfort |
| ex | from, out of, beyond | exchange, exclaim |

## Your Turn

**Find and circle five words with *de, dis*, or *ex* in the puzzle.**

```
e x c h a n g e d e x d r
x t o e d o d x e x o i e
d e o d i o m n i d i s a
e m e x c l a i m e d i s
r e d e d i s a g r e e d
e s d i s b e l i e f r e
```

**Use the circled words to complete these sentences.**

1. I _____ with Uncle Jim that the tent could be set up easily.

2. Then I watched in _____ as Uncle Jim pitched his tent in ten minutes.

3. I was trying to _____ the instructions when he offered to help me pitch mine.

4. We _____ jobs, and before long, the tent was up.

5. I _____ , "Wow! That wasn't so hard!"

**Underline the word that correctly completes each sentence. Write a meaning for the word you choose. Use a dictionary if you need help.**

6. I was at a (disadvantage, deadvantage), not knowing what to wear on the camping trip. _____

7. Some people (exbelieve, disbelieve) that a sweater is needed at high elevations, but it is. _____

8. You may see some (disformed, deformed) trees along some trails.
_____

9. These trees were attacked by a (desease, disease) that caused them to grow in strange ways. _____

10. If you packed frozen food, it might (disfrost, defrost) too soon.
_____

11. Sometimes you bring (exhydrated, dehydrated) food to eat on the trail.
_____

12. At the end of the day, you may sit around a campfire and (dechange, exchange) stories about your adventure. _____

**Editing** Read more about Brian's trip. Find and correct the spelling of eight words with prefixes.

| Mistakes | |
|---|---|
| Capitalization | 3 |
| Punctuation | 2 |

During our trip, we did a lot of exploring. We also did some fishing It was fun to stop by a clear blue stream and fish for our supper—except I didn't catch too many fish. I was surprised to discuver how much I liked hiking. my new hiking boots were uncomfturbul at first. That displeesed me greatly. But once I broke the boots in, my feet felt fine. We hiked up and down long mountain trails. sometimes we dissagreed on which trail to take. We dislyked our map because it was difficult to dekode. But, we never got lost! I saw all kinds of unuzual wildlife? I never detected any wild animals in my sleeping bag—although one day i did eksterminate a lot of hungry mosquitoes!

# SPELLING, PART 1

In each row, underline the word with a <u>long</u> vowel sound in the first syllable.

1. silent     solid     silver     summer

2. ferry     ferret     ferris     feline

3. label     larva     lapel     lasso

4. muffin     motor     morsel     money

5. honest     husband     human     helmet

In each row, underline the word with a <u>short</u> vowel sound in the first syllable.

6. baby     banjo     bone     broken

7. river     rival     rifle     rodent

8. metal     meteor     meat     media

9. mumble     music     muse     mutiny

10. rodeo     robin     robot     Roman

Divide these words into syllables.

11. basket _____     12. pillow _____

13. compile _____     14. motel _____

15. magnet _____     16. model _____

Add the ending shown to each word. Write the words on the lines.

17. hobby (es) _____     18. try (es) _____

19. monkey (s) _____     20. divide (ing) _____

21. dodge (ed) _____     22. cross (ing) _____

23. trim (ed) _____     24. hurry (ing) _____

Underline the word that correctly completes the sentence.

25. To prepare for the test, (preview, review) this lesson carefully.

26. I'm all thumbs! Will you please help me (pretie, untie) this knot?

27. Our dog (disappears, misappears) when it's time for his bath.

28. A rock is an example of a (reliving, nonliving) thing.

**Read each sentence. Circle the meaning of the underlined word.**

29. For a crispier pizza crust, <u>preheat</u> the oven to 400°F.

    heat beforehand     heat again     heat wrongly

30. If you don't understand the directions, please <u>reread</u> them.

    read wrongly     read again     read together

31. The directions were not well written; they were <u>unclear</u>.

    not clear     not clean     very clear

32. This is an <u>imperfect</u> pizza; the crust is burned.

    really perfect     almost perfect     not perfect

33. A biography is a work of <u>nonfiction</u>.

    pure fiction     not fiction     not factual

34. I think I <u>misspelled</u> the author's name.

    spelled wrongly     spoke wrongly     spelled correctly

35. My report on the book is <u>incomplete</u>.

    very complete     complete again     not complete

36. Will you help me <u>decode</u> this message, please?

    undo the code     put into code     code again

37. This sale is final; the shoes may not be <u>exchanged</u>.

    changed wrongly     unchanged     changed for others

38. I hope the shoes don't cause me any <u>discomfort</u>!

    lack of style     lack of comfort     lots of comfort

**A word is used incorrectly in each sentence. Cross out the incorrect word. Write the correct word on the line.**

39. I cried because the book had such an inhappy ending.

    _____

40. I need to preread that paragraph to find the supporting details.

    _____

41. Not having a list of spelling words puts me at a misadvantage.

    _____

42. "I won first prize!" reclaimed Henry. _____

NAME _____

# SPELLING, PART 1

Fill in the circle by the word with a <u>long</u> vowel sound in the first syllable.

1. ○ radar    ○ rabbit    ○ radish    ○ rascal
2. ○ metal    ○ monster    ○ mitten    ○ motor
3. ○ trigger    ○ tiger    ○ tingle    ○ triple
4. ○ mister    ○ mustard    ○ music    ○ master
5. ○ lemon    ○ legend    ○ legal    ○ letter

Fill in the circle by the word with a <u>short</u> vowel sound in the first syllable.

6. ○ puny    ○ python    ○ pupil    ○ public
7. ○ shadow    ○ slogan    ○ sneakers    ○ solo
8. ○ pony    ○ pilot    ○ petal    ○ photo
9. ○ silver    ○ soda    ○ solar    ○ silence
10. ○ vocal    ○ volley    ○ voter    ○ vibrate

Read the first word. Fill in the circle by its correct syllable division.

11. welcome    ○ welc • ome    ○ we • lcome    ○ wel • come
12. zebra    ○ zeb • ra    ○ ze • bra    ○ zebr • a
13. senate    ○ sen • ate    ○ se • nate    ○ sena • te

Fill in the circle by the word that is spelled correctly.

14. ○ typeing    ○ useing    ○ erasing    ○ deleteing
15. ○ rubys    ○ berries    ○ cherrys    ○ fairys
16. ○ hurried    ○ carryed    ○ marryed    ○ scurryed
17. ○ suning    ○ swiming    ○ skiming    ○ stopping
18. ○ swimer    ○ stoper    ○ bigger    ○ beger
19. ○ lilys    ○ buryed    ○ dryed    ○ trying
20. ○ replyed    ○ relied    ○ copyes    ○ pansys

**Fill in the circle by the word that correctly completes each sentence.**

21. We saw a _____ of the new movie.

    ○ misview    ○ preview    ○ nonview    ○ deview

22. Paula will _____ the desks.

    ○ inarrange    ○ exarrange    ○ rearrange    ○ nonarrange

23. In a spelling bee, you are out if you _____ a word.

    ○ respell    ○ dispel    ○ misspell    ○ expel

24. Have everyone in the group _____ their ideas.

    ○ prechange    ○ mischange    ○ unchange    ○ exchange

25. I was _____ of the large dog.

    ○ unafraid    ○ nonafraid    ○ misafraid    ○ disafraid

26. The puzzle was _____ to solve.

    ○ inpossible    ○ unpossible    ○ nonpossible    ○ impossible

**Fill in the circle by the sentence that uses the underlined word correctly.**

27. ○ After the children's party, the room was in <u>disorder</u>.

    ○ After the children's party, the room was in <u>reorder</u>.

28. ○ Moosehead Lake is an <u>inland</u> lake in Maine.

    ○ Moosehead Lake is an <u>imland</u> lake in Maine.

29. ○ The <u>prestop</u> flight got us there earlier.

    ○ The <u>nonstop</u> flight got us there earlier.

30. ○ In his story, the spy was <u>debriefed</u> after the mission.

    ○ In his story, the spy was <u>unbriefed</u> after the mission.

**Fill in the circle by the word that correctly completes each sentence.**

31. Dinosaurs _____ millions of years ago.

    ○ disguised    ○ diseased    ○ disappeared    ○ disappointed

32. Did you ever try writing with _____ ink? It's fun!

    ○ invisible    ○ indoor    ○ incorrect    ○ infield

NAME _____

# SCHWA SOUNDS

## Become a Super Writer

Tricia began writing an informative essay on raising a kitten.

*Before I got Sparkle, I didn't know how much work was needed to care for and raise an animal. But, as you will see, I did it!*

Say the underlined words in Tricia's sentences. Listen to the final syllable in each word. They all end with the same vowel sound, the **schwa-*l*** sound.

**Definition · Rules**

The **schwa sound** is the vowel sound you hear in unaccented syllables.

- The **schwa-*l*** sound can be spelled in different ways:
  *le* as in *sparkle*    *el* as in *cancel*    *al* as in *animal*    *il* as in *pencil*
- If you're not sure how to spell a word with schwa-*l*, look it up in a dictionary.

## Your Turn

**Write the correct letters to complete each schwa-*l* word.**

1. On my tenth birthday, my parents took me to an anim ___ ___ shelter.
2. A woman put a small bund ___ ___ of fur in my arms.
3. I couldn't believe this litt ___ ___ kitten was mine.
4. The woman told us sever ___ ___ things about caring for a kitten.
5. Then Dad lined a box with an old tow ___ ___ for the ride home.
6. Believe it or not, the ride home was pretty norm ___ ___ .
7. The kitten liked to cudd ___ ___ and slept the whole way.
8. Naming the kitten was pretty simp ___ ___ .
9. I called her Spark ___ ___ for her sparkling eyes.
10. Unfortunately, Sparkle managed to get into troub ___ ___ .
11. First, her collar got caught in the strap of Mom's sand ___ ___ .
12. Then she jumped on the kitchen tab ___ ___ .
13. She knocked part of Dad's breakfast bag ___ ___ off his plate.

**SPELLING 167**

**Use the clues below and a schwa-*l* word from the word bank to complete the crossword puzzle. Not all the words will be used.**

**Across**

1. a soft, chewy candy
4. a kind of tree
6. an underground passage
8. at the center
10. nearby or close
11. a cloth marker or tag
12. a breakfast food

**Down**

1. funny or amusing
2. small in size
3. a pattern for tracing
5. a writing instrument
7. a soft, warm material
9. a word puzzle
10. faithful and true

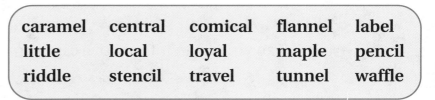

| caramel | central | comical | flannel | label |
| little | local | loyal | maple | pencil |
| riddle | stencil | travel | tunnel | waffle |

 **Editing**  Edit Tricia's paragraph about Sparkle. Look for and correct seven spelling errors in words with schwa-*l*.

| Mistakes | |
|---|---|
| Capitalization | 1 |
| Punctuation | 1 |

Cats can be hard to train, but I've learned that a lot of praise and littel morsils of food can help. For exampel, when sparkle sharpens her claws on the scratching post and not the carpet, I praise her, and she purrs. She has learned a coupl things on her own She figured out how to open the door on the stenceled hall cabinet. She also thinks it's great fun to knock pencils on the floor. It's comicul to see her come running whenever she hears a can being opened!

# SUFFIXES

## Become a Super Writer

George and his classmates put on a circus act for a local preschool. Some of his classmates wore animal costumes. Here is one of George's dialogue lines.

*For your <u>enjoyment</u>, our <u>fearless</u> animal trainer will now tame a lion!*

Look at the underlined words. Notice how the **suffixes** *ment* and *less* changed the meaning of the base words *enjoy* and *fear*.

### Definition · Rules

A **suffix** is a word part added to the end of a base word or root word to create a new word. Suffixes change how a word is used in a sentence. The new words can be used as nouns, verbs, adjectives, or adverbs. When you add a suffix, the spelling of the base word may change.

- Drop the final *e* before a suffix that begins with a vowel. *(live, livable)*
- Change the final *y* to an *i* before adding a suffix. *(happy, happiness)*
- Check the dictionary if you are unsure how to spell a word with a suffix.

## Your Turn

**Add the suffix to the base word in parentheses to complete each sentence.**

| SUFFIX | MEANING | EXAMPLE |
|---|---|---|
| able | able to be, can do | livable, readable |
| less | without | fearless, senseless |
| ness | the state of being | quietness, kindness |
| ful | full of | playful, useful |
| ment | the act or result of | enjoyment, government |
| ly | in the manner of, like | quickly, hastily |
| ion | the act or state of | procession, champion |

1. The ushers will _____ show you to your seats. (happy + ly)

2. The elephant works for a _____ of peanuts. (pay + ment)

3. Have you ever seen such _____ animals! (love + able)

4. As you can see, monkeys are _____ climbers. (skill + ful)

5. Even though snakes are _____ , they can be very fast. (leg + less)

6. For _____ sake! Don't tease the lion! (good + ness')

7. Aren't the feathers of the peacocks _____ ? (beauty + ful)

8. Speak _____ so the giraffe can hear you. (loud + ly)

9. This clown can give you _____ on how to be funny! (instruct + ion)

**Add** *able, less, ness, ful, ment, ly,* **or** *ion* **to the base word in parentheses to write a word that correctly completes each sentence.**

10. Our clowns will now perform for your _____ . (amuse)

11. Ha! This poor clown doesn't know which _____ to run. (direct)

12. The ostrich is _____ one of the biggest birds in the world. (easy)

13. Did you know that an ostrich is a _____ bird? (flight)

14. A net is a _____ tool for the trapeze bears. (value)

15. Watch these _____ bears fly through the air. (grace)

16. Can you believe the _____ of the elephant's skin? (thick)

17. We hope you had a _____ time. (wonder)

**Find in this puzzle the words you wrote above. Circle the words.**

```
W O N D E R F U L E T A
G F T H I C K N E S S M
D R I T H G L E S B E U
E V A L U A B L E I S S
A G R C C R C F U L S E
S D I R E C T I O N R M
I D R E A F I O N H E E
L U L F R D U R E E N N
Y F L I G H T L E S S T
```

 **Editing**   **Edit George's opening speech to the preschoolers. Underline and correct seven errors in words with suffixes.**

| Mistakes | |
|---|---|
| Capitalization | 2 |
| Punctuation | 2 |

Ladies and gentlemen and the children of Miss brady's class,

It is with great happiment that I am here? Today for your enjoyful, Mr. Walker's fifth-grade class will put on an unbelievely circus show. Now for anyone who might be afraid, let me say that all the animals are very friendness. They are lovable beasts. in fact, they are really harmly children in costumes! But they will do circus acts just like real animals. So sit quietful in your seats and have an enjoyable time! Let the actness begin

# ROOTS

## Become a Super Writer

Andy is making a book of riddles for his little sister. Here's a favorite of his.

Q: If a parrot were <u>speaking</u> to a frog, what might it say?

A: Polly wants a croaker.

The word *speaking* is formed by adding the ending *ing* to the **root** *speak*. You can add many word parts to this root to form new words.

**Definition · Rules**

A **root**, or base word, is a word or part of a word to which other word parts can be added. Adding word parts to roots forms new words with new meanings. Roots like *drink, speak, read,* and *happy* can stand alone as words.

• A root word's spelling does not change when a prefix is added.

• Adding a suffix or ending to a root word may change the spelling. See pages 155, 157, and 169 for help on endings and suffixes.

| |
|---|
| speak: speaks, speaking, misspeak, unspeakable |
| drink: drinks, drinking, drinkable, undrinkable |
| read: reads, reading, reader, readable, misread |
| happy: unhappy, happiest, happily, happiness |

## Your Turn

**Add a prefix, suffix, or ending to the word in parentheses to complete each riddle.**

1. Q: What did the _____ driver say to the wagon? (happy)

   A: Stop coaching me!

2. Q: I've been _____ your composition about your house. Why is it the same as your brother's? (read)

   A: My brother and I live in the same house.

3. Q: What kinds of _____ do boxers like best? (drink)

   A: They like fruit punches.

4. Q: How is a skyscraper like a _____? (read)

   A: Both have lots of stories.

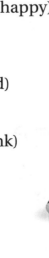
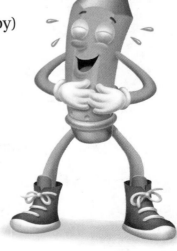

**Use the clues to complete the puzzle.**

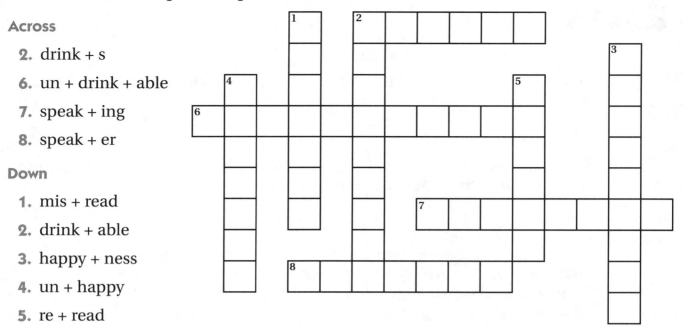

**Across**

2. drink + s

6. un + drink + able

7. speak + ing

8. speak + er

**Down**

1. mis + read

2. drink + able

3. happy + ness

4. un + happy

5. re + read

---

**Editing**   Edit Andy's paragraph. He used the wrong forms of *drink, happy, read,* and *speak.* Fix his seven errors.

| Mistakes | | |
|---|---|---|
| Capitalization | 2 |
| Punctuation | 2 |
| Spelling | 3 |

I like to read to my little sister. Sometimes, I write the books that I misread to her. My sister likes all kinds of books She is not a rereader yet, but she is a very good listener. unfortunately, she always wants to see the picktures. I must admit that i am not the world's best artist. I am happiness when I am writing. I do not derive much happily from drawing. Wuns I made a book of riddles for my sister. I had to draw a pikchure of a boxer drinks a glass of fruit punch. That was a real challenge? Perhaps if I misspeak to my mother, she will let me take some art lessons. Or better yet, perhaps I should be speaker to my sister. It's time for her to learn to read!

# COMPOUND WORDS

## Become a Super Writer

Look at the entry Tara made in her journal.

_Everyone_ in the _classroom_, all _twenty-six_ of us, was excited about the class trip to the _amusement park_.

Look at the underlined words in Tara's sentence. The words _everyone_ and _classroom_ are called **compound words**, or **compounds**. They are made by joining two smaller words. Some compounds, like _twenty-six_, are joined with hyphens. Others, like _amusement park_, are called open compounds.

**Definition · Rules**

A **compound word** is made up of two or more words used together as a new word. There are three kinds of compound words. Use a dictionary to check how specific compound words should be written.
- One-word compounds: _everyone, classroom, gumdrop_
- Two-word, or open, compounds: _amusement park, comic book_
- Hyphenated compounds: _twenty-six, pinch-hit_

## Your Turn

**Underline the two words in each sentence that form a compound, then write the compound correctly. If the words are correct as they are, write _correct_.**

1. I packed a drink, a snack, and a lunch in my back pack. _____

2. We put our packs in the over head rack. _____

3. One of my class mates forgot his lunch. _____

4. Our teacher said he could buy a hot dog at the park. _____

5. Betsy was nervous that the bus did not have seat belts. _____

6. The driver made an announcement on his loud speaker. _____

7. He said it would be a ride of forty five minutes to the park. _____

8. The ride was bumpy, especially on the high way. _____

9. When we pulled into the parking lot, we all cheered. _____

10. Then we asked where we could find the nearest bath rooms! _____

**In this word hunt, combine each word with another to form a compound word. Write three compound words on the lines.**

**11.** quarter     back     yard     stick

_____

**12.** ball     park     way     foot

_____

**13.** baby     sit     stairs     up

_____

**14.** week     light     house     day

_____

**15.** cake     ice     cream     cheese

_____

**16.** hill     touch     down     top

_____

 **Editing**     **Read more of Tara's journal entry. Fix six errors in compound words.**

| Mistakes | | |
|---|---|---|
| Capitalization | 3 |
| Punctuation | 2 |
| Spelling | 5 |

The first ride Betsy and I went on was the rollercoaster. Naturally, betsy

asked if they had seat belts. (Of course, they did!) Anyway, it was grate fun and

we screemed the whole way! After that hair-raising ride, we wanted some thing

quieter. we decided to try the merri-go round. It was a beautyful old-fashioned

ride with horses and stage-coaches going around in a circle. Betsy and I wanted

to ride in a stagecoach, but they were all taken. Instead, we picked out side-by-

side horses to ride? We asked mrs. O'Conner to take a snapshot of us on

horse-back. I can't wait for those picktures to come back

NAME _____

# HOMONYMS AND PROBLEM WORDS

## Become a Super Writer

Jeremy jotted down the definition of *mammal* as his teacher read it aloud.

*Any animals that have hair on <u>there</u> bodies and that produce milk for feeding <u>they're</u> young*

When Jeremy reread the definition, he realized that he had substituted the **homonyms** *there* and *they're* for the word he really wanted to use, *their*.

**Definition · Rules**

**Homonyms** are words that sound alike but have different meanings and spellings. Some sound-alike words cause problems because each one is used in a different way in a sentence.

• The spelling of a homonym should match the meaning that is right for the sentence.

• Check a dictionary if you are not sure which homonym to use.

| HOMONYM | USE | HOMONYM | USE |
|---|---|---|---|
| your | possessive pronoun | to | a preposition |
| you're | contraction of <u>you are</u> | too | means "also" |
| our | possessive pronoun | two | the number 2 |
| hour | a term for time equal to sixty minutes | their | possessive pronoun |
| its | possessive pronoun | there | means "at or in that place" |
| it's | contraction of <u>it is</u> | they're | contraction of <u>they are</u> |

## Your Turn

**Underline the correct homonym to use in each sentence.**

1. Its/It's true! An elephant and a mouse have something in common.

2. Is it there/their/they're big ears?

3. Well, they both have to/too/two big ears, but that's not it.

4. Is it the fact that there/they're both gray?

5. No, its/it's that they're both mammals.

6. Your/You're kidding, aren't you?

7. Our/Hour mouse will be surprised to meet its/it's cousin, Jumbo!

**Write a homonym from the box to complete each group of sentences.**

8. _____ are more than 900 species of bats.

9. And they are all mammals, _____ .

10. Most bats make _____ homes in the tropics.

| their | there |
|-------|-------|
| to    | too   |

11. The smallest bat is about the size of _____ thumbnail.

12. _____ the smallest known mammal in the world.

13. This bat makes _____ home in Thailand.

| its  | it's   |
|------|--------|
| your | you're |

14. _____ teacher says the largest bats live in Africa and Asia.

15. _____ wings spread out over five feet!

16. _____ called flying foxes and, luckily, eat only fruit.

| their | they're |
|-------|---------|
| our   | hour    |

17. _____ are about 40 species of bats in North America.

18. Although most bats are harmless, _____ better off not handling them.

19. _____ known to sometimes carry rabies.

| there | they're |
|-------|---------|
| your  | you're  |

20. A bat has to live with the myth of _____ blindness.

21. But bats really have _____ perfectly good eyes.

22. The dark of night makes it hard for a bat _____ see.

| its | it's |
|-----|------|
| to  | two  |

**Editing** Read Jeremy's description of mammals. Correct five errors Jeremy made in using homonyms.

| Mistakes | |
|----------|---|
| Punctuation | 2 |
| Spelling | 3 |

Mammals are members of the group of aminals with backbones, or spines.

There all species of animals that feed milk two their young. Did you know that

your a mammal just like a whale, a horse, or a bat. Mammals are warm-blooded

creetures. There hearts have four chambers just like you're heart. All mammals,

even whales and other sea mammals, must breath air

# Synonyms and Antonyms

## Become a Super Writer

Sonya found a report she had written when she was in the second grade. Here is how it began.

*Some dinosaurs were very big. Some dinosaurs were not very big.*

Sonya laughed when she read the sentences. She now knew that **synonyms** and **antonyms** could have made her writing more interesting. She could have used, for example, a synonym *huge* or *gigantic* to take the place of *big*. She could have used an antonym such as *small* or *tiny* to say the opposite or to replace the words *not very big*.

### Definitions

A **synonym** is a word that has the same or almost the same meaning as another word. Often, there are several synonyms for one word.

An **antonym** is a word that is the opposite or almost opposite in meaning to another word. Often, a word has more than one antonym.

If you need suggestions for various words' synonyms and antonyms, look through a thesaurus.

## Your Turn

**Write a more interesting synonym or antonym to replace the underlined word or words in each sentence.**

1. Some dinosaurs <u>ate</u> plants all day long. _____

2. Other dinosaurs <u>ate</u> meat in big bites. _____

3. *Brachiosaurus* had a long neck to <u>eat</u> the leaves off trees. _____

4. *Stegosaurus* ate low plants and had a <u>not very long</u> neck. _____

5. Some dinosaurs traveled in <u>groups</u>, like cows. _____

6. Some meat eaters traveled in <u>groups</u>, like wolves. _____

7. The <u>meanest</u> dinosaur was *Tyrannosaurus rex*. _____

8. One dinosaur that was <u>not mean</u> was *Maiasaura*. _____

9. *Maiasaura* was a <u>very good</u> mother. _____

10. The <u>meaning</u> of *maiasaura* is "good-mother lizard." _____

For each word below, find and circle a synonym and antonym in the puzzle. Write the words under the correct headings.

| Word | Synonym | Antonym |
|------|---------|---------|
| 11. beautiful | _____ | _____ |
| 12. difficult | _____ | _____ |
| 13. modern | _____ | _____ |
| 14. go | _____ | _____ |
| 15. fast | _____ | _____ |
| 16. tired | _____ | _____ |
| 17. take | _____ | _____ |
| 18. shut | _____ | _____ |

| P | A | C | L | O | S | E | H | F | S | L |
|---|---|---|---|---|---|---|---|---|---|---|
| R | R | B | P | P | E | E | A | S | W | A |
| G | H | E | H | E | U | A | R | L | I | R |
| Y | I | T | T | N | G | S | D | D | F | R |
| E | A | V | R | T | L | Y | L | L | T | I |
| S | L | E | E | P | Y | O | N | S | J | V |
| I | A | L | E | R | T | L | E | A | V | E |
| G | R | A | B | S | L | O | W | K | I | R |

 **Editing**  Sonya wrote a new dinosaur report. She underlined words she wanted to replace with stronger synonyms. She boxed a word she wanted to replace with an antonym. Replace these words for Sonya.

| Mistakes | |
|----------|---|
| Capitalization | 3 |
| Punctuation | 4 |
| Spelling | 3 |

"Dinosaur" is the comon name for two groups of reptiles that <u>lived</u> millions of years ago. Many dinosaurs were the <u>biggest</u> creatures that ever walked the earth. brachiosaurus was eighthy feet long. Tyrannosaurus rex was ten feet <u>high</u> at the hip and over forty feet long Its head reached a <u>width</u> of four feet, and when it opened its huge mouth, it displayed six-inch long, <u>sharp</u> teeth. Unlike people: Dinosaurs [always] stopped growing. They continued to <u>grow</u> in size until the day they died. that may explain why there are no more dinosaurs? Maybe, they just became two big!

# SPELLING, PART 2

Write *le, el, al,* or *il* to complete the unfinished words.

1. A fab ___ ___ is a short story.

2. It is usually quite simp ___ ___ , with few characters.

3. It has a mor ___ ___ , or a lesson.

4. An anim ___ ___ in the story has human qualities.

5. Lots of peop ___ ___ enjoy reading Aesop's stories.

6. Sever ___ ___ of you have read "The Tortoise and the Hare."

7. Some stories tell how the ev ___ ___ fox is outwitted.

8. You will marv ___ ___ at these characters' cleverness.

**Make a new word to fit each phrase by adding a suffix to the underlined base word.**

9. without a <u>clue</u>                    _____

10. capable of being <u>loved</u>            _____

11. state of being <u>inspect</u>ed          _____

12. full of <u>spite</u>                     _____

13. the act of <u>enjoy</u>ing               _____

14. in a <u>speedy</u> way                   _____

15. the state of being <u>happy</u>          _____

**Write the compound word suggested by the clue.**

16. the number of cents in a quarter       _____

17. where you go to catch an airplane      _____

18. to take care of someone's baby         _____

19. a very cold dessert served in a cone   _____

20. the two days at the end of the week    _____

21. a tall building that reaches high into the sky  _____

22. what you are when your feet are bare   _____

23. a fraction that names one piece in four  _____

24. a chair with wheels on it that assists the disabled  _____

**Underline the correct homonym to complete each sentence.**

25. It's/Its supposed to rain tonight.

26. I left my wallet at there/their/they're house.

27. Is he your/you're brother?

28. The watch was useless. It's/Its face was smashed.

29. When there are no clean clothes, Dave does our/hour laundry.

30. Grandma said there/their/they're not arriving until after dinner.

31. The bus is late, and I'm not sure when its/it's coming.

32. I'm short, but your/you're sister is tall.

33. When your/you're finished with the test, raise your hand.

34. His little brother is only to/too/two years old.

35. Can you come to my house in one our/hour?

36. Let's walk to/too/two school today.

37. Our/Hour teacher used to live in Rhode Island.

38. I've never been their/they're/there.

39. I have been to Illinois, Ohio, Indiana, and Kentucky, to/two/too.

40. There/Their/They're not far from Michigan, where I live.

**Write a synonym for each word.**

41. afraid _____
42. cry _____
43. happy _____
44. little _____
45. end _____
46. stop _____
47. funny _____
48. help _____
49. fast _____
50. fancy _____

**Write an antonym for each word.**

51. near _____
52. heavy _____
53. down _____
54. inside _____
55. enter _____
56. laugh _____
57. before _____
58. add _____
59. friend _____
60. cold _____

# SPELLING, PART 2

**Fill in the circle by the word with the correct schwa-*l* spelling.**

1.  ○ trouble ○ troubel ○ troubil ○ troubal
2.  ○ evel ○ evle ○ evil ○ eval
3.  ○ severil ○ several ○ severle ○ severel
4.  ○ cradal ○ cradil ○ cradel ○ cradle
5.  ○ medle ○ medal ○ medel ○ medil
6.  ○ gental ○ gentil ○ gentel ○ gentle
7.  ○ natural ○ naturel ○ naturil ○ naturle
8.  ○ circal ○ circel ○ circal ○ circle
9.  ○ novle ○ novel ○ noval ○ novil
10. ○ pickel ○ pickal ○ pickle ○ pickil

**Fill in the circle by the suffix that can be added to the underlined root word in each sentence.**

11. An umbrella gives you <u>protect</u> from the rain. ○ ness ○ ion ○ able

12. Your handwriting is so neat and <u>read</u>. ○ able ○ ness ○ less

13. The children playing on the playground were very <u>cheer</u>. ○ ment ○ ly ○ ful

14. The carrots were cooked so long they were <u>taste</u>. ○ less ○ able ○ ful

15. I'm sorry about our <u>argue</u>. Let's shake hands and make up. ○ ness ○ ment ○ ful

16. We spoke <u>soft</u> because the baby was sleeping. ○ ment ○ able ○ ly

17. My scissors won't cut through the <u>thick</u> of the cardboard. ○ ion ○ ness ○ ly

18. The principal made an <u>announce</u> over the loudspeaker. ○ ment ○ ly ○ able

19. The child played <u>happy</u> in the sand box. ○ ment ○ ly ○ able

20. The <u>play</u> puppy dragged the old sock. ○ ion ○ ful ○ ness

**Fill in the circle by the compound word that matches the definition.**

21. the sport that uses a ball and a hoop    ○ basket-ball    ○ basketball

22. two dimes and five pennies    ○ twenty five    ○ twenty-five

23. a room where you sleep    ○ bedroom    ○ bed room

24. what your mother's mother is to you    ○ grand mother    ○ grandmother

25. a light that helps to control traffic    ○ traffic-light    ○ traffic light

**Fill in the circle by the homonym that completes each sentence.**

26. When ____ raining, we play indoors.    ○ its    ○ it's

27. We went hiking ____ on our vacation.    ○ there    ○ their    ○ they're

28. We're going on a trip ____ the mountains.    ○ to    ○ too    ○ two

29. If ____ ready, we can leave now.    ○ your    ○ you're

30. ____ coming soon.    ○ There    ○ Their    ○ They're

31. The bird hurt ____ wing.    ○ its    ○ it's

32. Can you come to ____ party?    ○ our    ○ hour

33. I have ____ much work to do today.    ○ to    ○ too    ○ two

34. When is ____ birthday?    ○ your    ○ you're

35. Tomorrow it will be ____ turn.    ○ there    ○ their    ○ they're

**Fill in the circle by the synonym for the underlined word.**

36. <u>none</u>    ○ few    ○ nothing    ○ some    ○ several

37. <u>start</u>    ○ halt    ○ stop    ○ begin    ○ end

38. <u>well</u>    ○ healthy    ○ ill    ○ sick    ○ poorly

39. <u>right</u>    ○ wrong    ○ correct    ○ left    ○ false

**Fill in the circle by the antonym for the underlined word.**

40. <u>wet</u>    ○ hot    ○ damp    ○ dry    ○ cold

41. <u>high</u>    ○ tall    ○ low    ○ expensive    ○ rare

42. <u>poor</u>    ○ needy    ○ hungry    ○ sad    ○ rich

43. <u>dark</u>    ○ light    ○ dim    ○ black    ○ plain

# GLOSSARY

## ABBREVIATIONS

- An **abbreviation** is a shortened form of a title or some other word or phrase used to save time or space.

    Titles of people/respect: Mr., Mrs., Dr., M.D.

    Periods of time: B.C., A.D., A.M., P.M.

    | Days: | Sun. | Mon. | Tues. | Wed. |
    |-------|------|------|-------|------|
    |       | Thurs. | Fri. | Sat. |   |

    | Months: | Jan. | Feb. | Mar. | Apr. |
    |---------|------|------|------|------|
    |         | May  | June | July | Aug. |
    |         | Sept.| Oct. | Nov. | Dec. |

    (*May, June,* and *July* are not abbreviated.)

    Units of measure:  ft   in.   mi   oz   lb

    (Note that *in.* is the only measurement abbreviation that needs a period.)

- Use post office abbreviations for **state names in addresses.** Capitalize both letters. Do not use periods.

    | Alaska | AK | New Hampshire | NH |
    |--------|----|---------------|----|
    | Idaho  | ID | South Dakota  | SD |

- **Address, organization,** and **business abbreviations** are written with an initial capital and a final period.

    | Ave. | St.   | Hwy. | S.   | Tpke. |
    |------|-------|------|------|-------|
    | Co.  | Corp. | Inc. | Org. |       |

## ADJECTIVES

- An **adjective** is a word that describes a noun or pronoun.

    The <u>lovable</u> koala is called the <u>Australian</u> teddy bear. Its fur is <u>soft</u> and <u>thick</u>.

- An **article** is an adjective. The articles *a* and *an* refer to any one person, place, or thing. *The* refers to a specific person, place, or thing, and can be used with singular and plural nouns.

    *Marsupial* is <u>the</u> name for <u>a</u> mammal with <u>a</u> pouch.

    <u>An</u> opossum, <u>a</u> kangaroo, and <u>a</u> koala are all marsupials.

    <u>The</u> names of other marsupials include <u>the</u> wombat and <u>the</u> wallaby.

- **Demonstrative adjectives** describe nouns. *This* and *these* describe nouns that are nearby. *That* and *those* describe nouns that are far away.

    <u>This</u> opossum lives in North America.

    <u>Those</u> kangaroos jump higher.

- A **comparative adjective** compares two nouns or pronouns. It shows how two people, places, things, or ideas are alike or different. To compare two things, *er* is added to short adjectives, or the word *more* is used with the adjective.

    A kangaroo is <u>larger</u> than a wallaby.

    A kangaroo is <u>more powerful</u> than a koala.

- A **superlative adjective** compares three or more nouns or pronouns. To compare more than two things, *est* is added to short adjectives, or the word *most* is used with the adjective.

    The red kangaroo is the <u>largest</u> marsupial.

    It is the <u>most massive</u> of all kangaroos.

- Comparisons with special adjectives are made by using different words. *Good* is one such adjective. Use *better* to compare two things; use *best* to compare more than two.

    The kangaroo's leap was <u>good</u>.
    The second was <u>better</u>.
    The third was the <u>best</u>.

## ADVERBS

- **Adverbs** describe action verbs, adjectives, or other adverbs. Most tell *where, how,* or *when* an action happens; many end in *ly. Very* and *always* are also common adverbs.

    The bears at the zoo stayed <u>outside</u> in the rain. (tells *where*)

    The giraffe moved <u>slowly</u> through the grass. (tells *how*)

    The zoologist fed the leopard <u>immediately</u>. (tells *when*)

## ADVERBS continued

- A comparative adverb compares two actions. To compare two things, *er* is added to short adverbs, or the word *more* is used with the adverb.

  > The cheetah runs <u>faster</u> than the lion.
  >
  > The young gazelle eats <u>more often</u> than its mother.

- To compare more than two things, add *est* to short adverbs or use *most* with the adjective.

  > Of all the monkeys, that one climbs the <u>highest</u>.
  >
  > Of all the monkeys, this one screams the <u>most loudly</u>.

- A negative is a word that means "no." Use only one negative in a sentence.

  > The panther does <u>not</u> come down from the tree.

### Problem Adjectives and Adverbs

- The following adjectives and adverbs are often misused.

  real/very    *Real* is an adjective. Use it to describe a noun or a pronoun. *Very* is an adverb. Use it to describe a verb, an adjective, or another adverb.

  > Is that a <u>real</u> polar bear?
  > Grizzly bears are <u>very</u> large.

  good/well    *Good* is an adjective. Use it to describe a noun or a pronoun. *Well* is an adverb. Use it to describe a verb, an adjective, or another adverb.

  > Her appetite was <u>good</u>.
  > The panda ate <u>well</u> today.

## AGREEMENT WITH ANTECEDENTS

A pronoun must agree with the noun it replaces. (An antecedent is the noun to which a pronoun refers.)

> The <u>star</u> was bright, and <u>it</u> twinkled in the sky.

## ANTONYMS    *See* Synonyms and Antonyms.

## APOSTROPHE

- An apostrophe signals letters that are missing in a contraction. It also signals ownership, or possession.

  > <u>it's</u> = it is, it has
  > <u>we're</u> = we are
  > <u>don't</u> = do not

- Add an apostrophe and *s* ('s) to form most singular possessive nouns, even those that end in *s*.

  > the <u>teacher's</u> class
  > the <u>class's</u> homework
  > Ms. <u>Jones's</u> new puppy

- Add an apostrophe (') to form possessives of plural nouns that end with *s* or *es*.

  > the <u>students'</u> seats
  > the <u>classes'</u> assignments

- Add an apostrophe and *s* ('s) to form the possessives of plural nouns that do not end with *s*.

  > the <u>men's</u> downhill race
  > the <u>sheep's</u> wool

## ARTICLES    *See* Adjectives.

## BASE WORDS AND ROOTS

A base word, or root, is a word or part of a word to which other word parts can be added.

> <u>happy</u> + ly = happily
> <u>swim</u> + ing = swimming

## CAPITALIZATION

- Capitalize the first word of a sentence.

  > <u>T</u>he sun sets in the west.

- Capitalize important words in proper nouns and proper adjectives.

  > the <u>U</u>nited <u>S</u>tates of <u>A</u>merica
  > <u>M</u>ayan art

- Always capitalize the pronoun *I* and contractions made with it.

    I'll    I'd    I've    I'm

- Capitalize the names of people and their initials.

    Susan B. Anthony    J.F.K.

- Capitalize titles of people.

    President Roosevelt
    Ms. Chen

- Capitalize historical events, documents, and periods of time.

    Boston Tea Party
    Declaration of Independence
    Middle Ages

- Capitalize days, months, and holidays.

    Saturday    July    Independence Day

- Capitalize abbreviations of titles and organizations.

    B.S. (Bachelor of Science)
    F.D.A. (Food and Drug Administration)

- Capitalize important words in organization, association, and team names.

    Boy Scouts of America
    the Republican Party
    National Football League

- Capitalize the first words of the opening and closing of a letter.

    Dear Elizabeth,    Sincerely,

- Capitalize geographic names.

    Mars; Iowa; North America; British Columbia; Fairfield County; Atlantic Ocean; Washington Memorial; Interstate 95; White House

- In titles of books, magazines, movies, and songs, capitalize the first and all the important words, plus all forms of *be*. Capitalize headlines the same way.

    The Lion, the Witch, and the Wardrobe
       (book)
    Aladdin (movie)
    Bulls Win Championship Title (headline)

- Capitalize the first word of a direct quotation or dialogue.

    Tommy shouted, "That water is cold!"

- Capitalize names of religions, nationalities, and languages.

    Islam, Buddhism, Christianity; French, Indonesian; Irish

- Capitalize names of businesses and their products.

    Pizza Hut, Wheaties, Aim toothpaste

 ## CLAUSES

- A **clause** is a group of words that has a subject and a predicate.

- An **independent clause** can stand alone as a sentence.

    While they were traveling westward, <u>they saw many Native American objects</u>.

- A **dependent clause** cannot stand alone as a complete sentence.

    <u>While they were traveling westward</u>, they saw many Native American objects.

 ## COLON

- Use a **colon** after the greeting, or salutation, in a business letter.

    Dear Mr. Fox:

- Use a colon between numbers to show time.

    10:00 A.M.

- Use a colon after names to show different speakers' words in a drama or play.

    MARK: Quick, let's get out of here!
    ANNA: But it's freezing outside!

 ## COMMA

- Use **commas** in dates.

    The concert will be Tuesday, June 2, 1998, in the gym.

- Use commas in addresses (but not between the state and ZIP code).

    The address is 2857 North Lake Drive, Milwaukee, Wisconsin  53201.

## COMMA continued

- Use a comma to make numbers easier to read (but not in years: 1950, 2000, 2020).

  *My mom bought a red sports car for $10,000. It has only 25,000 miles on it!*

- Use commas to set off mild interjections or interruptions.

  *My, what a beautiful dog!*
  *It was, however, a long walk home.*

- Use a comma and a conjunction in a compound sentence.

  *I have not washed my car in a week, yet it still looks shiny.*

- Use a comma to set off dialogue or quotations.

  *Walt Disney said, "If you can dream it, you can do it."*

- Use a comma in direct address.

  *Jean Marc, is that you?*
  *Watch out for the puddle, Michaela!*

- Use a comma after the greeting and closing of a friendly letter.

  *Dear Grandma Beth,        Yours truly,*

- Use a comma to separate items in a series or list of three or more things.

  *Kevin had hot fudge, whip cream, and a cherry on his ice cream sundae.*

- Use a comma to separate two or more adjectives not joined by a conjunction.

  *He ate the sweet, delicious sundae in less than a minute!*

- Use a comma to set off phrases or clauses when they begin a sentence.

  *After Kevin polished off the sundae, he got a stomachache.*

 ## COMPOUNDS

- A **compound word** is made up of two or more words used together as a new word.

| Closed | Open | Hyphenated |
|---|---|---|
| rainbow | polar bear | ninety-nine |

 ## CONJUNCTIONS

A **coordinating conjunction** joins two or more words, phrases, or simple sentences. Coordinating conjunctions include *and, but, or, nor, for, so,* and *yet.*

*The batter was not nervous <u>or</u> afraid.*

*A curve ball was thrown, <u>yet</u> the batter hit a home run.*

## CONTRACTIONS  *See* Apostrophe, Problem Words.

 ## DIRECT OBJECTS

A **direct object** receives the action of the verb. It may be a noun or a pronoun.

*The pony express riders encountered many <u>dangers</u>.*

*The riders overcame <u>them</u>.*

 ## ENDINGS AND SUFFIXES

- An **ending** or a **suffix** is a word part added to the end of a base word or root to create a new word. The ending or suffix may also change the spelling of the base word.

- If the base word ends in *e*, drop the *e* before an ending that begins with a vowel.

  dive + ing = diving
  confuse + es = confuses
  dance + ed = danced

- For most words ending in *e*, keep the *e* when adding an ending or a suffix that begins with a consonant.

  use + ful = useful
  hope + less = hopeless

- If the last syllable of a word ends with CVC (consonant-vowel-consonant), double the last consonant when adding *ed, ing, er,* or *est.*

  win + er = winner
  begin + ing = beginning
  hot + est = hottest

- For words that end with a consonant + *y*, change the *y* to *i* before adding an ending. Notice the exception when the suffix begins with *i*.

  happy + ness = happiness
  worry + ed = worried
  marry + ing = marrying

- If a word ends with a vowel + *y*, add the ending without changing the base word.

  stay + ed = stayed
  monkey + s = monkeys

 ## EXCLAMATION POINT

Use an exclamation point after an exclamatory sentence, interjection, or phrase.

Stop!    Happy Birthday!    It's Friday!

 ## HOMONYMS AND PROBLEM WORDS

- Homonyms are words that sound alike but have different spellings and meanings.

| | |
|---|---|
| *its/it's* | Our cat chases <u>its</u> tail. |
| | When trees bud, <u>it's</u> time for spring. |
| *your/you're* | What happened to <u>your</u> clothes? |
| | <u>You're</u> covered in mud! |
| *there/their/* | Hang the picture over <u>there</u>. |
| *they're* | Who forgot to put <u>their</u> name on the test? |
| | <u>They're</u> going to the playground. |
| *our/hour* | We left <u>our</u> map at home. |
| | We are already an <u>hour</u> late. |
| *two/to/too* | I would like <u>two</u> scoops of ice cream. |
| | I want to bring this sundae <u>to</u> my mom. |
| | I'd like some hot fudge, <u>too</u>. |
| | That's <u>too</u> much hot fudge! |

 ## HYPHEN

- Use a hyphen to connect words or numbers that act as one word.

  sister-in-law          twenty-one

- Use a hyphen to divide a word at the end of a line.

 ## INDIRECT OBJECTS

An indirect object tells to whom or for whom an action is done. It may be a noun or a pronoun.

Many people send <u>friends</u> letters by mail.

## INITIALS   *See* Abbreviations, Period.

## NEGATIVES   *See* Adverbs.

 ## NOUNS

- A noun is a word that names a person, place, thing, or idea.

- A common noun is a general name for a person, a place, a thing, or an idea.

  woman    store    cities    happiness

- A proper noun is a name for a specific person, place, or thing. Proper nouns are capitalized.

  Antarctica    Ghandi    Chicago Bulls

- A singular noun names one person, place, thing, or idea.

  sister    building    box    match

- A plural noun names more than one person, place, thing, or idea. Many plurals are formed by adding *s* or *es*:

  sisters    buildings    boxes    matches

- An irregular plural noun names more than one person, place, thing, or idea. It does not end in *s* or *es*:

  foot/feet    woman/women    moose/moose

- A possessive noun shows possession, or ownership. *See also* Apostrophe.

## OBJECT OF A PREPOSITION

*See* Prepositions.

## PARENTHESES

Use pairs of **parentheses** to set apart extra information within sentences.

> The message says to call my mom ASAP (as soon as possible).

## PERIOD

- Use a **period** at the end of a statement or a command and after initials and abbreviations.

> It is raining outside.     Take an umbrella.
>
> R.S.V.P.                        T.M.

- Use a period as a decimal point in numbers.

> 98.6°F          $9.99

- Use a period after Roman numerals and capital letters in outline parts.

> I. A.

## PHRASES

- A **phrase** is a group of words that has meaning but that does not express a complete thought.

- An **adjective phrase** works as an adjective to describe a noun or a pronoun.

> My friend toured mountains <u>in the West</u>.

- An **adverb phrase** works as an adverb to tell more about a verb.

> I traveled <u>to the Pacific Ocean</u>.

- A **verb phrase** works as a verb to tell more about the noun.

> Worms <u>can be found</u> under most rocks.

## PREDICATES

- The **complete predicate** consists of the simple predicate and all the words that make up the predicate part of the sentence.

> Riders <u>changed ponies frequently</u>.

- The **simple predicate** is the main verb in the complete predicate.

> Pony express riders <u>earned</u> $100 to $150 in a month.

- A **compound predicate** consists of two or more simple predicates joined by *and* or *or*.

> They <u>climbed</u> mountains, <u>crossed</u> rivers, and <u>galloped</u> through the desert.

*See also* Sentence Parts.

## PREFIXES

A **prefix** is a word part added to the beginning of a base word or root.

> <u>un</u> + happy = unhappy
> <u>non</u> + sense = nonsense
> <u>im</u> + mobile = immobile

*See also* Base Words and Roots.

## PREPOSITIONS

- A **preposition** is a word that relates a noun or a pronoun to another word in the sentence. Some common prepositions are *about, after, at, beside, by, down, during, for, from, in, into, like, over, under, with*.

> The batter stood <u>beside</u> home plate. He glared <u>at</u> the pitcher.

- The **object of a preposition** is the noun or pronoun that follows the preposition.

> The team tensely waited in the <u>dugout</u>.

- A **prepositional phrase** is a group of words that begins with a preposition and ends with a noun or a pronoun.

> The fans cheered loudly <u>from the stands</u>.

## PROBLEM WORDS

- The following words are often misused.

| | |
|---|---|
| *sit/set* | *Sit* means "rest or stay in one place."<br><br>Let's <u>sit</u> down in the circle.<br><br>*Set* is a verb meaning "put."<br><br><u>Set</u> the glass in the sink. |
| *may/can* | *May* is used to ask permission or to express a possibility.<br><br><u>May</u> I have a scoop of chocolate? I <u>may</u> go to the movies.<br><br>*Can* shows that someone is able to do something.<br><br>I <u>can</u> easily eat three scoops of ice cream. |
| *doesn't/don't* | *Doesn't* is used with singular nouns and the pronouns *he*, *she*, and *it*.<br><br>Patrick <u>doesn't</u> like peas.<br><br>*Don't* is used with plural nouns and the pronouns *I*, *you*, *we*, and *they*.<br><br>The <u>children</u> <u>don't</u> know the route. |

*See also* Homonyms and Problem Words; Adverbs.

## PRONOUNS

- A pronoun takes the place of one or more nouns. Personal pronouns include *I*, *me*, *you*, *he*, *him*, *she*, *her*, *it*, *we*, *us*, *they*, and *them*.

- A subject pronoun is used as the subject of a sentence. Subject pronouns are *I*, *you*, *he*, *she*, *it*, *we*, *you*, and *they*.

  <u>Carl</u> likes astronomy. <u>He</u> studies the stars through his telescope.

- An object pronoun is used to replace a noun that follows an action verb or after words such as *to, for, in,* or *with*. Object pronouns include *me, you, him, her, it, us,* and *them*.

  Carl pointed to the <u>Big Dipper</u>. Carl pointed to <u>it</u>.

- A possessive pronoun shows ownership. Some possessives come before the noun.

  This is <u>his</u> telescope.

- Possessive pronouns, such as *yours, mine, theirs,* and *ours* stand alone.

  This telescope is <u>his</u>. <u>Hers</u> is over there.

- A demonstrative pronoun identifies a specific person, place, or thing. The demonstrative pronouns are *this, that, these,* and *those*.

  <u>This</u> is the best way to get there.
  <u>That</u>'s my Uncle Edwin.

- Interrogative pronouns, such as *who, what, which,* and *whose,* can be used to ask questions.

  <u>Who</u> can find the Big Dipper?
  <u>Which</u> planets make up our solar system?

## QUESTION MARK

Use a question mark after interrogative sentences that ask direct questions.

Would you like to come over to my house?

## QUOTATION MARKS

- Quotation marks set off quotations and titles.

- Use quotation marks for titles of songs, poems, short stories, essays, chapters of books, and articles found in magazines, newspapers, or encyclopedias.

  "The Star-Spangled Banner" (song)
  "Paradise Lost" (poem)

- Use quotation marks before and after a speaker's exact words.

  "Look," said Jane. "There's a rainbow in the sky."

**ROOTS**  *See* Base Words and Roots.

## SCHWA SOUNDS

- The **schwa** sound is the vowel sound you hear in unaccented syllables. The /ə/ + *l* sound can be spelled in different ways.

  *le* as in *double*　　　*al* as in *signal*
  *el* as in *funnel*　　　*il* as in *stencil*

## SENTENCE PARTS

A **sentence** has two main parts, the complete subject and the complete predicate.

  <u>Many riders</u> carried the mail in leather saddlebags. (complete subject)

  Many riders <u>carried the mail in leather saddlebags.</u> (complete predicate)

*See also* Subjects, Predicates.

## SENTENCES

- A **sentence** is a group of words that states a complete idea.

- A **simple sentence** expresses one complete thought.

  Tanya enjoys American history.

- A **compound sentence** has two or more simple sentences joined by a comma and a conjunction, such as *and, but, or, nor*.

  She reads books on history, <u>and</u> she visits historic places.

- A **complex sentence** includes a simple sentence and one or more clauses that cannot stand alone.

  <u>While he served as president</u>, Thomas Jefferson encouraged westward expansion. (Idea cannot stand alone.)

  While he served as president, <u>Thomas Jefferson encouraged westward expansion.</u> (Idea can stand alone.)

### Kinds of Sentences

- A **declarative sentence** makes a statement.

  The Eagles shot the winning basket.

- An **interrogative sentence** asks a question.

  What was the final score?

- An **exclamatory sentence** shows surprise or strong feeling.

  I can't believe they won!

- An **imperative sentence** gives a command or makes a request. The subject *you* is understood.

  Please move down a seat.
  Bring back a hot dog and a soda.

## SUBJECTS

- The **subject** names someone or something and usually does something.

- The **simple subject** is the main noun or pronoun in the complete subject.

  The fastest <u>journey</u> covered 2,000 miles in seven days.

- The **complete subject** includes all the words that tell whom or what the sentence is about.

  <u>Brave people on horseback</u> rode well.

- A **compound subject** has two or more simple subjects that have the same predicate and are joined by the words *and* or *or*.

  <u>Horses</u> and <u>riders</u> have traveled far.

**SUFFIXES**  *See* Endings and Suffixes.

## SYLLABLES

- A **syllable** is a word or part of a word. Every syllable has a single vowel sound. A closed syllable ends in one or more consonants. An open syllable ends in a long vowel sound.

- If a two-syllable word has two consonants in the middle, divide the word between the two consonants.

  nap • kin　　　tim • ber　　　blan • ket

- If a two-syllable word's first syllable has a long vowel sound, divide after the first vowel.

  spi • der　　　vi • rus　　　na • ture

- If a two-syllable word's first syllable has a short vowel sound, divide after the middle consonant.

    tim • id          dam • age          crit • ic

## SYNONYMS AND ANTONYMS

- A **synonym** is a word that has the same or almost the same meaning as another word.

    <u>big</u>: huge, large, gigantic, immense, vast

- An **antonym** is a word that is opposite or almost opposite in meaning to another word.

    <u>cool</u>: warm, balmy, hot, heated, tepid

## TENSES

- **Tense** tells when the action of a verb takes place. Use the same tense for all verbs in a sentence or paragraph, unless a **change of tense** is needed to make the meaning clear.

- The **present tense** states an action that is happening now or one that happens regularly.

    Peter <u>builds</u> boats.
    He <u>is sailing</u> up the coast in a race.

- The **past tense** of a verb states an action that already happened.

    Connie <u>sailed</u> yesterday.
    She <u>was excited</u>.

- The **past tense of regular verbs** is formed by adding *ed* or by adding *ed* and using the helping verb *have*.

    I <u>sailed</u>.          I <u>have sailed</u>.

- The **past tense of irregular verbs** are formed in different ways.

    I <u>see</u> the boat.
    Earlier I <u>saw</u> the boat.
    I <u>have seen</u> the boat.

- The **future tense** states an action that will take place in the future. It is made by using the helping verb *will* or *shall* before the main verb.

    We <u>will sail</u> to Bermuda next weekend.
    I <u>shall pack</u> my bags.

## UNDERLINE AND ITALICS

- Use **underline** or **italics** to show the titles of books, plays, newspapers, magazines, television programs, movies, CDs, audiocassettes, and other complete works.

    *The Lion King* or <u>The Lion King</u> (play)
    *World of Nature* (TV program)

- Use **italics** to show stage directions in play scripts.

## VERBS

- A **verb** shows the action in a sentence. It tells what the subject does, or it links the subject to another word in the sentence. The verb is the main word in the predicate.

- An **action verb** tells what action the subject does.

    The gymnast <u>tumbles</u> across the floor.

- A **linking verb** connects the subject of a sentence with a noun or an adjective in the predicate. It tells what the subject is or is like.

    The gymnast <u>is</u> an athlete.
    The gymnast <u>seems</u> energetic.

- A **helping verb** helps state an action or show time.

    She <u>was</u> swinging back and forth on the uneven bars.

    She <u>will</u> win the gold medal.

- A **singular verb** is used with a singular subject.

    She <u>practices</u> every day.

- A **plural verb** is used with a plural subject.

    Jen and John <u>practice</u> every day.

## You UNDERSTOOD   *See* Sentences.